Experience Life 1
The Window of Wonder

"You often hear people talk about the power of the spoken and written word. Yes, words and descriptions are immensely powerful, but they are a poor substitute for the experience itself. A seldom talked-about property of words is that they cannot convey the essence of experience. *The Secret Way of Wonder* urges the reader to travel beyond mere words into a realm of intensely personal experience where the description becomes part of conscious perception. With compelling logic, this book outlines an interactive and experiential method for asking questions we may have been afraid to ask before: to *wonder* if there isn't a better way than falling into the same tired reactions, to *wonder* if there is a higher level of awareness above our old problems, to question our belief that settling a disturbance solves the disturbance once and for all. Simply asking the question with a wondering attitude places us in a position to receive the genuine answers.

"*The Secret Way of Wonder* gently guides the reader to self-discovery and to the revelation that through a 'window of wonder' life can begin to take on a fresh and authentically exciting quality."

—**Dr. Lynne D. Franklin**
psychologist

About the Author

Son of Larry Finley, the late-night talk show pioneer and celebrity, Guy Finley began his spiritual writings when he was 14 years old. He has had numerous successful careers. His songs have been recorded by many Motown artists, and he has worked in television and motion pictures both as composer of musical scores and actor. After a soul-searching trip to India and the Far East in 1979, he gave up his career to simplify his life. He helped found the nationally recognized self-development program, "Success Without Stress." He now travels and lectures nationwide on the principles of Higher Life.

To Write to the Author

We cannot guarantee that every letter written to the author can be answered, but all will be forwarded. Both the author and the publisher appreciate hearing from readers, learning of your enjoyment and benefit from this book. Llewellyn also publishes a bi-monthly news magazine with news and reviews of practical esoteric studies and articles helpful to the student, and some readers' questions and comments to the author may be answered through this magazine's columns if permission to do so is included in the original letter. The author sometimes participates in seminars and workshops, and dates and places are announced in *The Llewellyn New Times*. To write to the author, or to ask a question, write to:

Guy Finley
c/o THE LLEWELLYN NEW TIMES
P.O. Box 64383-221, St. Paul, MN 55164-0383, U.S.A.
Please enclose a self-addressed, stamped envelope for reply, or $1.00 to cover costs.

The Secret Way of Wonder

Insights from the Silence

Guy Finley

Introduction by Desi Arnaz, Jr.
Foreword by Dr. Ellen B. Dickstein, Ph.D.
Special Message from Vernon Howard

1992
Llewellyn Publications
St. Paul, Minnesota 55164-0383, U.S.A.

FIRST EDITION
Second Printing, 1992

Cover design by Christopher Wells

Library of Congress Cataloging-in-Publication Data

Finley, Guy, 1949-
    The secret way of wonder : insights from the silence / Guy Finley
        p.   cm.
    Includes index.
    ISBN 0-87542-221-7
    1. Wonder. 2. Life. 3. Meditations. I. Title.
BJ1595.F56   1992   92-2920
158' .1—dc20   CIP

Llewellyn Publications
A Division of Llewellyn Worldwide, Ltd.
P.O. Box 64383, St. Paul, MN 55164-0383

Printed on recycled paper.

What you want also wants you.

If you seek the celestial,
the celestial also seeks you.

There are no unanswered requests
in the universe.

If we do not like what we
are receiving, we can
learn to ask for something different.

Then we will find what we wish.

—Vernon Howard

Also by Guy Finley

Success Without Stress (not available from
    Llewellyn Publications)

The Secret of Letting Go

CONTENTS

Introduction

by Desi Arnaz, Jr.

When Guy and I were teenagers, our first meeting was probably nothing unusual. We were two young men full of ourselves and our dreams for the future. Through music, both of us shared a common love. But as we got to know each other better, there was something else we both shared—something indescribable—a longing for the Truth—the Truth about everything and about why life was the way it was.

Why and how are we the way we are? Who or what created all of this that we see? And all that we don't see? Is there a God? Are there other worlds that lie yet beyond our imagination? Through our "wonder years," both of us searched endlessly for the answers to these spiritual questions. Sometimes glimpsing a part of the puzzle, we would excitedly tell our "story" to the other or try to express our insight regarding something that we had experienced or understood. But there was always more to the experience that we could not express with words, no matter how hard we tried. We both agree that what we learned from this was one of the most important insights we have ever had. The insight was that the description of the experience is only that—a description—it could never be the actual experience. There is always something more that we cannot put into words. The explanation of the experience is not the experience.

In my early teen years, I had a math tutor who was a UCLA math student. He was also a friend of mine from childhood. One day, while explaining a geometry question, we started talking about mathematical theory—things like the fact that there is no end to measurement whether it be the largest number or smallest. With the use of telescopes and microscopes, scientists have discovered objects they never knew existed before. But no matter how well we can see physically, even with instruments that make the seemingly invisible visible, there will always be something smaller and larger than what we are seeing now. The mathematical fact of this is presented in this way: If you are five feet away from a wall and walk one-half the distance each time you take a step, you will never reach the wall! My friend went on to say that some math students, after hearing this open-ended, eternal fact, quit math for good because they couldn't stand the fact that there is always more to see. Or put in another way, this is not why they wanted to study math. Oh no, life is infinite, with no beginning and no end! Therefore, Reality is not something that can be experienced by merely describing it, or thinking about it. This shocking revelation changes everything!

My intellect cannot find for me what I'm truly looking for, which is to experience eternity. Even my imagination can't give me this state of wholeness or fulfillment. Therefore, this sense of "wonder" is all that we have to probe the limitless expanse of the universe within us and outside of ourselves. All the mind can do is form a description of what we see, but in Truth, all that we are and all that we see in the visible and invisible world is beyond words. The only way to experience the "wonder" of the infinite is to be a part of it. For example, I can tell you about the unbelievable workings of nature, or the ocean, or how water tastes, or what it's like to go surfing or scuba-diving. But unless you experience it for yourself, my description of the ocean will never even come close to the experience. The description of the thing is not the thing! It's just a description.

"Wonder." The way that I am using that word, is not imagination, but rather an attention—a looking at what is going on inside and outside. It's an attention to all the thoughts and feelings one may have. It's looking at everything with a keen interest to learn what is its True Nature.

Guy's book helps to explain how to use "wonder" in order to see what is True about ourselves and also what is not True. The greatest adventure a human being can go on is the inner journey of self-discovery. With the power of Honesty and a sense of sincere "wonder," we can look at how the inner-life works and how the mind and emotions operate in our daily lives. We can discover what is beyond our present understanding. Let's journey together, along with my friend, Guy Finley, as he helps us to help ourselves awaken to the power of "wonder" in order to truly have a wonderful life!

Foreword

by Dr. Ellen B. Dickstein, Ph.D.

Freud once commented that when he passed through the streets of Vienna and saw all the stolid and somber citizens of the town, he wondered what had happened to all the delightful children. Have you ever really looked at the faces of the people around you? Watch them in the street, standing in line, eating in a restaurant. Watch them when they should be having fun, when they're Christmas shopping, or waiting for a movie to begin. The expression on the face reveals everything about the quality of the life. Have courage and really look.

When you look at the face of the average person at odd moments you will see dull eyes and a fixed expression. The body may be sitting in the chair, eagerly awaiting the arrival of the first course of a gourmet meal, but that sparkle of awareness, of true pleasure in life—of wonder—is not there. Observe how the mouth tends to fall into its accustomed mold. For one person it might be a tight line of discontent; for another a vacant looseness; for a third a complacent little smile, belied by the flashes of anger that pass across the eyes at unguarded moments.

The hardest test of all is to catch our own face in the

mirror when we have not had a chance to arrange it into its favorite "mirror expression." It can be a shock when we first realize how years of pain and disappointment have etched themselves into the corners of the eyes and the set of the chin. If this had to be our permanent state it would be wrenching to see it. But this is the wonderful part. Our very willingness to see that we have lost something vital in life is the first step to regaining it. The true realization of what we have let slip away brings the desire for its recovery. And just as a few drops of pure water awaken the dormant plant so that it sends out tiny roots in search of more water, so the first hints of the possibility of a new kind of freshness and energy lead to the desire for greater and greater change, until the entire life is transformed.

In order to experience that transformation we must start where we are, with the fact of our present pain and confusion. And we must try to understand how we got here in the first place. What has happened to strip us of our joy of life? Why do our days fall into patterns that bind like entangling nets? What weighs us down and anchors us to the life that we can see, so that we never look to the possibilities that lie beyond it? And what are those possibilities? We each can, and must, find the answers in ourselves. But we can't do it with our old ways of thinking about things. We need help.

The Secret Way of Wonder provides help. It is a very different kind of book that teaches the reader how to make contact with that part hidden within himself that already knows how to think about things in a new way. The book can serve as a meditational tool that focuses our wondering so that the process unfailingly yields new insight. It is an interactive spiritual workbook, offering guided practice for self-study. *The Secret Way of Wonder* provides the reader with the basic knowledge he needs to start searching for the lost knower within, an opportunity and encouragement to actually make several sorties on his own, and a technique that can be used again and again, leading to continued progress for years to come.

But all this takes time and effort. Why is it necessary? It is because finding that hidden knower, the higher self, is the most important thing anyone can do. But it is also the most difficult. Perhaps the story of a woman will explain why. She could be any woman, or any man. She could be you or me.

There once was a woman whose life was full of heartache. She did everything she knew to try to make it better, but no matter where she went, or what she did, nothing ever changed. If she got tired of one apartment she would move to another. But before long she would be tired of it in the same way. One relationship with a man would turn sour, so she would find another. But before long, the new relationship would turn sour in the same way. Sometimes when she grew weary of all her plans and activities a nagging feeling would come to her that unless something completely new *happened to her*, nothing would ever change at all.

Now there was something very interesting about this woman. When she was a young girl her mother gave her a diary and told her that if she wrote down her experiences and feelings every day, the book would become a companion to her for life. The little girl did as she was told. Every day she wrote down what had happened. Soon she found it comforting not only to write down her experiences, but to re-read what she had written before. As she nervously faced the challenges of each new day she would consult her diary to see how she had handled such things in the past. As she repeated each action it became more deeply ingrained in her character. As her diary grew, her picture of herself became stronger and more hardened, while the boundaries of possibility in her life became more and more narrow.

This is where we find her right now. She believes that her diary keeps her safe. Its wisdom is her guide through each day. She cannot see that by consulting her diary she simply perpetuates the mistakes of her past. The "wisdom" of her diary is nothing more than the accumulation of actions she had once taken by chance alone. Her life never changes because she is always forcing it into the artificial mold of what has come before. Rather than keeping her safe, her diary puts her in the greatest danger of all—the danger of never discovering who she really is, of why she is here on earth—the danger of never making a connection with that Higher universal force that had provided her with the very essence of her life to begin with, and that can never be found within the small, repetitive whirlpool of her own mind. This is the story of all of us, although we may not have a physical diary to show for it. The diary is within us. We have tried to make ourselves secure by hanging on to the familiar, and in so doing we have cut ourselves off from everything that makes life worth living. The only chance any of us has is to put the diary away and never consult it again. We must see through the false and stale answers we have given ourselves all these years, and make contact with something new and helpful, something that really cares for us, something that lies beyond the pages of the book we have written.

I always like happy endings. The woman in our story finally throws away her diary and starts off on a truly new life. We all have the opportunity to do the same, and *The Secret Way of Wonder* points the way. It helps us to ask the right questions, and teaches us how to find real answers in a new place. What an exciting and life-healing journey we have embarked upon when we have seen the futility of our old path, and are willing to strike out upon the untried yet true. What wonderful vistas open before us as fresh breezes blow from the endless source of all that is vital and new. This is what life is all about. This is what has eluded the masses of humanity. This is the great gift that awaits all who will reach for it through the window of wonder.

****

Dr. Ellen Dickstein, Ph.D., Psychologist, received her doctoral degree from John Hopkins University in Baltimore, Maryland. She taught at the university level, earning tenure at Southern Methodist University in Dallas, Texas. Ellen's research on the development of personality and the self-concept has been published in professional journals such as *Human Development, Journal of Personality and Social Psychology, Developmental Psychology* and *Journal of Consulting and Clinical Psychology*.

Choosing The Way Of Wonder

A Special Message From The Author

There is a powerful boyhood memory of mine which tells a story about two distinct Paths we can take through this life. This book is all about one of those Paths: the one called Wonder. And what we are going to learn from our work together is how to walk along this Wonderful Way. Let's begin.

On the surface, that evening didn't seem to be anything extraordinary. As usual, my family was entertaining some important guests from out-of-town. At the time, all of us were seated around a well-appointed and spacious dining room table in a private room of an exclusive restaurant. Food, drinks and talk were everywhere.

I wasn't exactly enjoying myself and I guess my preoccupation must have been out on my sleeve. The next thing I knew, I had attracted the unwanted attention of one of my father's friends.

At the moment he spoke to me, I was in deep (as deep as a child of 10 or 11 can go), deep thought. I was wondering why adults felt the need to spend so much time talking. Even at that age, it was clear to me that most of the answers they arrived at—about this or that— never really amounted to much or changed anything. Surely there had to be something more important to do with our lives than what this evening—and all other evenings like them—had to offer. I was beginning to Wonder.

The man's words broke into my distance and dragged me back to the smoky, talk-filled table.

"You don't look like you're enjoying yourself too much," he said, with that smile adults get when they know you aren't enjoying yourself.

"No, I'm not," I half-smiled and replied. I didn't really care what he thought.

"What seems to be the problem?" But I knew he truly didn't want to know. He wasn't even looking at me anymore.

I decided to tell him the answer anyway; at least as best I could. Choosing my words I began. "There has to be something more to life than this," I continued as earnestly as I knew how. "Don't you ever wonder about what we're meant to do with our lives—about the reason for being alive? Don't you feel like you're here FOR something?"

I'll never forget to this day what happened next—because something I said must have struck the man somewhere he didn't like. Suddenly I had his full attention. Only, right at that moment, I was wishing I didn't.

His face went deadly serious and it lost its color. He started talking with a strange urgency. It was clear he was straining to make an impression on my young mind. He made an impression all right, but nothing like what he had intended.

"Listen to me, young man," he said. "When I was your age I too used to wonder about all of those things—the why's and the wherefore's. But I can tell you, all you're doing is wasting your time. Forget it, believe me—I know!" After looking once around the table to make sure he wasn't missing out on anything of importance, he went on with his wisdom. "There are no answers to those kind of questions you have. All you're going to do is drive yourself crazy. Relax—learn to enjoy what you have. Just look around you—you're a lucky boy!"

There was no way for me to understand at the time exactly what I saw that night, or why the impressions that flooded into my young being seemed so powerful. But now I know. I was feeling a new and strange kind of sorrow. Now I know I had sensed, even back then, that Wonder had died in that man. And with its passing had also passed away the only chance he would ever have to make contact with a Higher world within himself; a Superior inner Realm without whose Wonders and Insights he would be left alone, locked inside a world of his own making. Without Wonder his days were charted to be spent as a weary wanderer in a closed world where the only answers he could ever hope to find would never be any Higher than his own.

Together, with this book and the healing Insights it will teach you to teach yourself, we are going to chart a brave, new and exciting course in favor of truly limitless living. We will discover the secret of how to contact the powerful, calm, spontaneous, friendly, and Wise forces of the OTHER world—that Higher, Truer world which can only be reached along the Path of Wonder. And best of all, our journey into this wonderful world within will reveal to us that EACH step we take in WONDER is really taking a step away from worry. So the farther we are willing to go, the happier we become! Let's be on our way.

I came upon two Paths and chose the one less traveled. That choice has made all the difference.

—Robert Frost

Chapter 1

The Secret Of Wonder And How It Works For You

I'm going to let you in on a tremendous secret about an invisible force powerful enough to change your world as you know it. At first you may be surprised. You may even disbelieve it. And that's just fine. One of the very first things you will learn about this Secret Force is that it works for you whether or not you believe in its power.

We are talking about working with Wonder.

Wonder is a window to a new and Higher world right within yourself. In this lofty, invisible realm, revealing insights and spontaneous intuition are the constant channels of communication by which you come to know the answers to all of your heart's desires. Revelation, not repetition is the commonplace. You know you live in a friendly, intelligent and Living Universe. And best of all, you know that you can reach into it and it can reach you—all through Wonder.

Sound too good to be true? I assure you working

1

with Wonder is all of this and more! I know. But before we can start to receive these Wise and Wonderful instructions from our Higher Nature, we must first make room for their arrival. The common and the Celestial cannot share our attention any more than a true king and a peasant can share ownership of a royal castle. We must choose which condition we wish to embrace. We must choose either Wonder's way—or our own. The following insights will help us to choose in favor of Wonder, which turns out, ultimately, to be the same as choosing in favor of our own True Self.

Wonder is a natural need: The gentle expression of our wish to meet and somehow understand the Intelligence which we sense surrounds us but that we can't see. It is through Wonder that we seek what we hope is seeking us. So we Wonder about love and Life's meaning. Where is it? What is it? Or is it at all? We Wonder about the stars that fill a night's endless sky—and then Wonder if our Wondering somehow reaches them—and if it does, to what avail? And we Wonder about the pain that turns our faces to the heavens for an answer, even as we Wonder about who we are and why do we exist?

So Wonder wells up within us from the heart. It is an unspoken question, an expectation of a safe, but still far-away shore. It is fueled by a longing, our natural need to close the gulf between what we feel and what we have yet to understand; and nothing short of this inner-union can satisfy this Higher calling. That's why any True Wonder we may have is ultimately answered in the form of revelation. We've all shared in a few of these Wonderful moments where suddenly it's as though we have new eyes or ears; where the whole picture comes to us and, as it does, because of our newly enhanced understanding, all conflict ceases. We see into the Truth of the matter. And to whatever extent that may be, we are that much more free than we were a scant heartbeat before.

There are no limits to Wonder. We can go just as high, be just as free as we need to. This is the key to harnessing the unlimited power of Wonder. It is the power of *NEED*. But, there is a vast difference between what we need and what we think we want. Please work extra hard to grasp the following few points.

The mind can only want what it thinks it needs. These mental needs are really just wants, and each of these desires lives only as long as the stimulation that temporarily brings it to life. Then it fades out of existence only to be replaced by another haunting want. For instance, we think we need others to approve us. This is not a real need. This is a want that always betrays us because no matter what we do, we never seem to get enough approval. And this want is the driving force which causes us to compromise our own integrity—as we sell ourselves for a smile. No one needs to compromise their Spirit. Here's another view of this same vital insight.

We all know that wants never seem to get satisfied. What we don't know is why. This is a Wonderful question. And like all questions Wonder is allowed to ask, we receive surprising, but substance-filled, answers. Let the following insight further our need to exchange our wants for new Wonders. It is impossible for the object of the want to satisfy the wanter because *the wanter is not real!* The wanter is only a sensation-packed thought-form anxiously seeking present contentment through the breathless pursuit of a past pleasure. Past and present can never meet. Wanter and Wanted cannot marry. Happiness is always denied. But this needn't be our sad story.

Unlike the wants of the mind, what the heart needs cannot be denied. This is the Secret of Secrets. The Living Need itself is proof that the thing needed already exists—and that it exists right now and within your reach! Could you need water if it's refreshing and life-giving qualities weren't something you had to have to live? Or, could you need sunlight if it's warmth and nurturing nature weren't already shining down on you? Of course not. What these valuable insights mean to us is that *our need is the connection to the thing needed.* Try and see this as fully as possible. Everything you really want depends upon it. The greater our need to live limitlessly, the surer will be our success.

And so THE question is—and always has been: How do we awaken this cosmically planted need-seed within? This question brings us to a crucial crossroad in our study of how Wonder works and how to make it work for us.

I'm sure you'll agree when we are feeling happy we don't spend our time Wondering how to be happy. That wouldn't make sense. We ARE happy and happiness doesn't seek itself. When our relationships are sailing along smoothly, we don't Wonder how to keep them afloat. We just enjoy the cruise and the fair seas that seem ahead. In these conditions we don't need happiness or emotional stability because we have it—at least for the moment. And that's just the point we need to investigate. Right beneath most of our happiness is the dim but definite realization that, like all the other happinesses we've ever known, this too shall pass. Now, whatever else we may do with this last idea, we mustn't push it away as being negative. I promise you we are on to something Wonderful.

It is not negative to admit we haven't been able to find lasting love—or contentment—or that our best solutions for ending self doubt have failed to produce security. On the contrary. This rare and honest self appraisal is the most positive step we can take for our own best, True interests. Why? Because this new kind of self honesty about our present condition, whatever it may be, awakens in us the need for what we know in our hearts we are meant to have and to be. Need is the infallible impetus. Wonder is the bridge. Let's take a quick look at how all of this works in our favor.

When we will at last allow ourselves to Wonder about some sadness or concern we've not been able to remedy, we are admitting, in however a small way, that we are no longer certain about even which questions to ask—let alone what answers to be looking for. Wonder's response—to this conscious self suspension of ours—is a new kind of sweetness that comes and washes away the bitterness of our seeming defeat. It does this each and every time when it shows us that the true solution, which it has now revealed to our weary eyes, was never to be found where we were looking for it in the first place! This is not only real relief, but real rescue as well. So Wonder works for us when we let our need ask for what *it* wants. Again, our need knows what it needs—which is, more often than not, totally different from what we think we want.

For instance, when we are worried over wanting others to like us, we tend to think that what we need is to dress snappier, be funnier, or to somehow become more powerful. But, if we were able to see that each of these kind of mental answers, our self serving solutions, have never delivered any real relief, we could then start to let go of them in favor of Wonder. Once we take this daring step away from our usual self and our certainty of what it is we think we want, then it is our need that begins to ask, to Wonder, which way is out?

Remember, this True Need knows that part of our new need is to see our whole problem in a new light—and that part of the very problem all along has been our unconscious belief that we understood the nature of our problem!

For instance, in the case of wanting peer approval, wonder reveals we never needed others to hold us in high esteem. And that's why, even when we may have received the applause, we were never any less anxious or worried. The real problem all along was that we were clinging to a weak and shaky part of ourself that believed without approval it would cease to exist. Yes, this is an unexpected answer. But the best has yet to come. Included in our Wonder-spawned insight is now the further NEED to stop serving this weakness. This is Strength! This is the Way Out.

Can you see the difference? With Wonder the answers we need are revealed, *not* the answers we think we want. Eventually, as we learn more and more to let Wonder have its Way with us, there becomes less and less distance between the answers we think we want and the Healing Insights we really need. This is True Harmony. This is the end of conflict.

When we Wonder we are willing to:

1. Suspend our own conclusions

2. Leave space for what is New

3. Relax in pleasant quietness

4. Trust in something Higher

5. See beyond ourself

6. Let Go

7. Need without knowing

8. Invite Intuition to instruct

9. Allow our heart to hear

10. Let something Wonderful in

There comes a Time when, on one hand a vague Awakening stirs the soul, the consciousness of a Higher Law ... and the sufferings a man endures from the contradictions of life, compel him to renounce the social order and to adapt the New. And this time has now arrived.

—Tolstoy

Chapter 2

Open The Window Of Wonder With These Amazing Insights

When we think to ourselves, "How else could I have handled that?", we are feeling the vague stirrings of Wonder. Just in asking the question, we can observe how at least a small part of ourself realizes, in hindsight, there had to have been a better, more intelligent way to have dealt with the disturbance in mind. And so, in almost each of our encounters with life's challenges or diversities, we also meet a moment where we somehow *know* or intuit there IS a superior way for us to BE. But it is here that we meet an almost unexplainable paradox.

This momentary window through which we see the possibility of a Higher State of Being for ourself, only opens to us in the light of that fleet instant when we realize—in some small way—the inadequacy or the weakness of our last response. This window is the ledge of Wonder. To stand before its opening is to shake consciously at all you may now see beneath you—the anger, the fears, the shadows of endless doubts—all of which gave rise to that weakness now visible before our inner eyes.

But, this same window also looks up and out upon an open and Higher World; a Supreme Realm that is free from all sad and self-punishing states. Our entrance into this new world depends solely upon the choices we make each time we stand before this window of Wonder. A few true-to-life examples will help bring these amazing new ideas into better view.

Maybe we're the kind of person who loses our temper when someone challenges our authority, but we're tired of coming apart when tugged on unexpectedly. Besides, we're starting to suspect that coming unglued may mean we're not as together as we would like to think. And so we begin to Wonder ... is my angry indignation a strength to call on, or could it be this "strength" of mine is actually a weakness? And could it be that this misunderstanding on my part is the only force that has ever been pulling on me?

Or perhaps in a moment of fear or frustration, we say something cruel to a friend or loved one. Maybe we thought that person we depended on was about to reject us. And so, rather than be hurt, we lash out to protect ourself by taking the first strike. WE do the rejecting. And in doing so, we create the very loss we had feared. Then comes that moment, that window in the midst of our unhappiness, where we find ourselves Wondering if just maybe we weren't betrayed a long, long time ago by something within our *own* self—and maybe that's why we have to keep going through these same sad scenes. Suddenly, and yet for perhaps the thousandth time, we know in our hearts that we need to have done differently than we did. And something else is also quite clear at that instant. We don't know how to *do* different—because we don't know how to *be* different!

Now, for a moment, that powerful need is there; and for that moment, the window of Wonder appears. We are aware we must change our being and equally aware we don't know how. Tremendous forces are awakening in us. We feel their powerful, disturbing presence.

But right at this critical juncture in time when the window of Wonder is wide open—and all of the real elements needed for true self-transformation have temporarily assembled—there is one evil element which always leaps through this special portal to spoil the potential of this magical mix. Fear rushes in.

Fear follows our need to be New like a hungry lion stalks a young gazelle. It can't afford to let us escape and it lurks about us precisely because it senses we are near the truly New. Do your very best to see the Truth of the following short summary: In that momentary Higher awareness, when we can clearly see we don't really know how to elevate our own life above our old problems, this moment produces both the need for self-newness—as well as the fear of it! This is the moment of Truth. And we must learn how to choose in favor what is New. Any other choice is made by fear.

How do we make this True, new choice for ourself? By refusing to select in favor of what seems *fa-*

miliar. Here's the explanation to this unusual but Wonder-producing fact.

The fear within us knows it must quickly find a way to place in check our awakening feeling of needing the new. It senses our temporary receptivity to this call of the Cosmic Life. It knows if our Wonder should go on unchallenged, we may soon begin to Wonder why we ever let fear have any say in our life at all! And so to shut the window on the possibility of this true deliverance, fear quickly but deftly offers us its own familiar solutions to settle our inner doubts and self-uncertainty. Here is how to recognize these seemingly attractive, but window-closing answers. They are always *circular*. We repeat them over and over again because these familiar answers come to us from *the same low level that produced our problems in the first place*.

Now comes an even more important lesson. These familiar solutions never solve our troubles, they merely settle them. And there is a vast difference. Settling a disturbance is *not* solving it—unless we still believe that diving under the covers after we hear a bump in the night has the power to quiet our trembling heart. It doesn't. Our under-cover shaking continues because this—and all other familiar but self-deceptive solutions—fail to reveal the real problem. And what we won't face, we can't erase.

It may be helpful at this point in our studies to shed some light on a few of the more common circular solutions to which we all still cling. The clearer we can make it for ourselves that these solutions are certifiably circular, the sooner we will be able to let them go! And in the space left by their absence, comes this crucial need for something New—comes the window of Wonder.

You may wish later on in your own workings with Wonder to expand this list. I urge you to do so. But, for now, take all the time you may need to Wonder about each of these next few examples. For extra helpful benefits, try to mentally connect them with some of the unresolved and repetitive problems in your life. As you work along from this point, do your very best to remember that Wonder is always *Light* in both senses of the word. So, don't fall into feeling sad, sorry, or stupid. Who you really are never suffers over any inner shadow, no matter how dark its appearance. To help you with all of this, here's a little reason-in-rhyme to keep fresh in mind as we continue on our inner journey:

> *Wonder Reveals*
> *What Fear Conceals*

Now, let's take a look at some of these hidden circular solutions.

Ten Circular Solutions

1. Saying "I'm sorry"

2. Denying the condition

3. Accepting defeat

4. Planning revenge

5. Explaining endlessly

6. Assessing blame

7. Calling yourself worthless

8. Feeling victimized

9. Getting angry

10. Hoping tomorrow changes

Now to this list of empty answers-in-action, let's add a few of their uniquely compelling characteristics. I have added a special insight following each one to help us make the right resolve to stop going round and round.

CIRCULAR SOLUTIONS ARE ALWAYS ...

1. Immediately Available:
All of our mental and emotional reactions are a continuation of the disturbance—and therefore, can never be its solution. Reactions are never solutions.

2. Effortless To Do:
It always feels easier to be carried along, but momentum is a most deceptive form of mindlessness. A rock rolling downhill gathers force, but its repeated collisions prove it has no choice in its direction.

3. Comforting By Nature:
The temporary comfort of clinging to what we think we know about the problem is almost always betrayed by the fact it was this same think-

ing that placed us in jeopardy in the first place!

4. Subtly Self-Serving:
The only problem with starring in your own mental movie is you never want the show to end—so you stop caring about the kind of roles you are given to play.

5. Certain In Their Direction:
We are never so lost as when thoughtlessness tells us which way is best to proceed.

The time has arrived for us to take the next step in our preparation to receive something Wonderful. Together, we have revealed and collected many powerful and fascinating facts about the world of Wonder. Now we must put all of our insights to work in our favor.

Religion has for centuries been trying to make men exult in the Wonders of creation, but it has forgotten that a thing can not be completely wonderful so long as it remains sensible.

—G. K. Chesterton

Chapter 3

Let Wonder Show You How To Shatter Painful Patterns

We've seen that as long as we allow our True needs to be answered by the familiar, we are going to live out our lives making unseen circles. We need to go UP, not around. There is another way to state this new and upward inner direction. What we really need is to make contact with that Higher part of our own True Nature which alone has the power to reveal ourself to our Self. Self discovery *is* self elevation.

There are no paths to this spontaneous realm of perfect understanding. And this is just one of its sublime mysteries. Here's another. No one is its visitor. Instead, when all is in order, when all is right and readied within, it visits us. And when it arrives, it reveals within us the one gift only it can bring: Self Harmony through Higher Self Understanding. So we can already see that learning to work with Wonder is unlike anything we may have ever tried to do before. Its uncommon and Celestial course is governed by lofty spiritual principles which often make no sense to our everyday mind. For instance, when it comes to working with Wonder, our ultimate success is determined by *what we don't do*.

Let's examine this unusual idea about inaction. For this study, we should recall what we learned before—about the intelligence of forsaking familiar solutions that merely settle our questions in favor of New and True insights which have the capability to actually solve them. Keeping this in mind, our lesson here is that when working with Wonder, one of the first actions we *don't* take toward a difficulty or heartache is to tell ourself what to do about it!

This brings us to an excellent place to stop for just a moment. There is something very important I want you to understand. And I know the following to be true. Many, many times along our way to what is Higher through Wonder, we will encounter what appears to be a hopeless dead-end. Confusion and doubt will cloud our minds and it will seem as though there is no way out. Don't buy into this hellish hoax.

This temporary scary inner condition is not only all right, but it's essential for our spiritual growth. How else could we make the Wonderful discovery that only when we come to the end of ourself—and all of our self created answers—that we meet the beginning of something that *isn't* us! This is the beauty and incomparable magic of Wonder. What we need is to be touched by something that isn't a part of our hidden circle of self. And a necessary part of establishing this contact comes with making it crystal clear to ourself that anything which directs us from our self-circle is part of why we stay dizzy and in the dark.

The idea of this hands-off approach to self-solving may seem a bit unsettling at first consideration. But, even a brief glance—at what must be seen as undeniable self evidence—will support our decision to embrace this new kind of spiritual non-action. Let the following special facts serve to confirm our suspicions.

1. We don't know the *real answers* or we wouldn't repeat the same problems.

2. We don't know the *real problems* or we wouldn't keep arriving at the same empty solutions.

It is crucial we be reminded—as often as possible—of the Goodness that comes to us each time we will dare to take this kind of honest self inventory. Why is it good to make ourself conscious of our present painful position? Because it is our unawareness which delivered us there in the first place. And our habitual answers are all a part of the unconscious patterns which leave us imprisoned. It should follow then: The clearer we can make this realization to ourself—that we don't know how to solve the circular, sad situation in our lives—the more we will be able to rev up our resolve to stick to our new resolution of *not doing* what we think we should.

Placing this new and true understanding of ours before our mechanical mental tendencies to always return to the known proves to be an exciting and Wonder-filled challenge; a lot like suddenly finding

yourself both the immovable object *and* the irresist-
ible force! Our new inner position—of taking no action toward our dilemma—will seem like it places us
between a rock and a hard place. Have no concern.
Again, this state is both good and necessary. The uncomfortable inner sensations of feeling squeezed is
born out of realizing that we need a solution to our
growing self concern, but realizing at the same time
that we must not allow our usual thinking to supply
the answer. In other words, we NEED to know, but
we know we don't! This moment is the one we have
been trying to avoid all our life—not having the quick
answers to put matters right—or seeing we don't
know the direction to take to reach real safety.

Everything we have been learning together
about Wonder is meant to deliver us to this precise
psychic point. And remember, we must not do anything about it. Any self rescuing action we would be
moved to take before this Window of Wonder will
only close it. Psychologically speaking, we must be
willing to remain right there boldly looking out into
what appears to be a great nothingness. But, if we
will stand there and Wonder—instead of turning to
worry—something unthinkable will happen right
before our inner eyes. To our eternal amazement, we
will see what we had believed to be the fearful unknown was really the Intelligent Unlimited.

This self-liberating discovery happens each and
every time we will bear with Wonder those anxious
periods when we feel as though the world is closing
in on us. I promise you, the only thing getting tighter
is our own circle of unconscious thoughts and feel-

ings we have unknowingly agreed to call our self. It is our Wonder-born insight that sees into this circle and that shatters it with its Light. Consider the freedom contained in the Light of this following insight: The uncomfortable sensation of feeling like you will be squeezed out of existence if you don't take some familiar action *only feels like it is happening to you*. It isn't!

This sinking feeling comes from and belongs to that limited low level within us which knows it must turn our eyes away from Wonder's window. It knows if it can't make you reach for one of it's sparkling but confused conclusions, it's only a matter of time until Wonder will reach your consciousness with a confusion-clearing and self illuminating Insight. Happiness and revelation arrive in the same instant.

> *The best way to come to truth being to examine things as really they are, and not to conclude they are, as we fancy of ourselves or have been taught by others to imagine.*
>
> —John Locke

Chapter 4

Here Is The Wonderful Seed Of A New Kind Of Strength

Never be afraid to Wonder. Never limit yourself to what you can Wonder about. Whatever your NEED to know may be, turn it over to Wonder and step back. You will receive an answer.

Real Wonder has no fear and fears nothing. Let your Wonder wander as far and as deep as it may wish to go. And then let it take you even further!

With each new insight gained, you will naturally Wonder what else there is waiting within you; what else can be revealed? In this way your inner life, your True Life, will begin to open up before you. And with increasing daily certainty, you will come to realize that your life was always meant to be a voyage into the New.

But there is one caution along our Way which must be mentioned. Otherwise, we are likely to fall for one of fear's most perilous deceptions. Please pay extra close attention to the following strange spiritual fact. Unlike other dangers—which may arise *because* we do something risky—the only danger to us on the road to a Wonderful new life comes from *not* taking risks! And there's more. Watch how this unusual idea grows clearer for us as I explain just what it is we must be willing to risk. The risk you and I must dare take is to laugh in fear's face and—in spite of its dark attempts to convince us otherwise—we must give ourselves permission to Wonder about our own weaknesses.

Please make the proper mental note that the author didn't say to go ahead and feel badly or shame-filled. And I don't mean to accept some embarrassed or self- sorry inner state. What I said was to Wonder about our weakness. This means to begin living with that intimate and unspoken question that comes with knowing that we don't know how to be strong—and that we NEED to.

So just go right ahead. Give yourself full permission to Wonder about *that* weakness, whatever form it may take. Wonder about being always weary or why you worry so; about your heavy heart or nagging fear; Wonder about the cruel thoughts and thoughtless acts—those jealousies and bitter feelings; Wonder about resentments and regrets, about anxiety and the anger that never doubts itself. Go ahead and dare to Wonder about ANY painful self-defeating habit you sense weakens you and ruins your days. DON'T BE AFRAID OF IT! Maybe you talk too much or you can't make a friend. Maybe you always feel betrayed. Whatever the doubt may be, put it to Wonder and watch what happens.

It is vital for you to understand these instructions are not asking you to dwell on the negative. They are not. Unknown to ourself, we are actually already doing just that each time we resist the conscious awareness of any self compromising inner state. This Higher insight is just one of the reasons Jesus Christ gave his disciples the beautiful but little understood spiritual direction that they should, "resist not evil." He was trying to teach those with ears to hear that their weakness *wasn't really their weakness at all*—but it was their fear of it that made it seem so. This is one of those impossible-to-understand-with-the-mind concepts whose meaning only Insight can reveal.

My favorite spiritual author, Vernon Howard, sheds much needed Light on this lofty and ever-deepening principle of "resist not evil" with these seven powerful words: **"Resistance to the disturbance is the disturbance."**

What this means in our study is once we begin to prefer Wondering *about* a weakness more than we want to live with and deny the secret worrying that comes *from* it, that weakness' days are numbered. This is the Truth. And this is what fear doesn't want us to know. But now we do. So let's follow this powerful idea all the way to its happy ending.

Most of us would agree, we would much rather forget a self flaw than favor it with our attention. But trying to forget a weakness is like trying to forget right in the middle of a storm that you never got around to fixing the hole in the roof. The point is obvious. There is no "forgetting" a weakness. And anything within our psyche that would urge us to close our eyes and ignore that we have been spiritually compromised is just another part of that same weakness. It knows the continuance of its non-life depends upon our unconscious agreement to help it stay out of sight and out of the Light. We can learn to do much better. Let's pause at this point to make an important inner connection.

Do you remember what we learned about the difference between settling a disturbance and solving it? The connection to be made here is that learning to Wonder about any self weakness is the same as inviting the healing insights we need into it. Each of these special self discoveries leaves us much stronger. Here's why. As we are willing to Wonder—and allow insight to bring us closer and closer to seeing the real inner *cause* of that weakness—we have also drawn closer to that Higher Intelligence whose Light first revealed this weakness—and whose very Presence will mean its eventual end. This is authentic self solving. Our reward is greater and greater self unity.

Sure, our secret fears whisper and sometimes shout that it's dangerous for us to dwell here—standing before this open window of Wonder. But in Truth, all we are really being asked to do is chance losing our constant, unseen uncertainty. Seen from this Higher vantage point, the question suddenly sounds a lot like wondering whether we should risk giving up a headache!

But fear has even more scary tactics up its dark sleeve to keep us full of worry instead of Wonder. The father of all that is weak, fear also wants us to believe that if we make our hidden inner tremblings conscious, it will be the same as resigning ourselves to a life of ceaseless shaking. This is simply another of its shameless lies. Nothing could be further from the rescuing Truth. Consciously admitting a weakness, and then remaining aware that we don't know what to do about its punishing presence, is *not* signing our name to a declaration of self failure. Just the opposite is True! Constant consciousness of any weakness is the seed of a new strength. Try and see the Truth and Goodness in this for yourself.

Our willingness to stay aware of whatever our weakness may be is the same as remaining conscious of our NEED for a strength NOT OUR OWN. This new and conscious NEED of ours is really the same as Conscious Prayer. And if we will not yield to the temptation of answering it ourself—with *our* ideas of what it means to be strong—then this need will know its answer. Then, and only then, we will at last have ours. This is the Great Mystery. The true strength we need always arrives. But it is never, never what we imagined. And that's the Wonder of it.

He who learns the rules of Wisdom, without conforming to them in this life, is like a man who labors in his field, but did not sow.

—Saadi

Chapter 5

Cross The Bridge Of Wonder To A Brand New Life

Whenever the subject of how to work with Wonder is brought up in one of my lectures or classes, it always raises many interesting and Wonder-provoking questions. And, as we will soon discover, my answers concerning Wonder more often than not leave the students with more questions than they started with! This approach is a bit unsettling at first, but everyone involved in these lively discussions knows that learning to live with Wonder is essential to their spiritual health and development.

I felt it would be extra helpful if we approached this summary chapter section with a review of some of these insightful questions and answers. As I said, you may find yourself Wondering about parts of the following exchange, but if this happens, just make a note, mental or otherwise, and return to it later on with new Wonder.

Question: It feels like I have so many needs. How do I know which ones are true and which are just wants that taunt?

Answer: Our true needs are really very simple— the Need to be kind, to be free, to be strong, to be spiritually wise, to know love. These real needs are self completing. The more they fulfill themselves, the more complete we are. On the other hand, our wants, even when answered, tend to leave us always *wanting* more.

Question: At one point, you said our success with Wonder depends on what we don't do. This instruction makes sense when it comes to not repeating self defeating circular solutions. But how does this unusual idea tie into Wondering itself? Are there areas of Wonder I shouldn't enter?

Answer: With Wonder, everything depends on where we are standing inwardly. Remember, true Wonder is borne from our understanding there is something we *don't* know—but that we Need to—if we are ever to find lasting contentment and happiness. This means that while we ARE seeking new solutions, we mustn't dare try and name them. The following examples will help reveal this important difference.

It is always spiritually wise to:

1. Wonder why things do or don't change—but not if they will.

2. Wonder about yourself—but not from yourself.

3. Wonder what lies beyond the known—but not into the known.

4. Wonder with every expectation—but not for the expected.

5. Wonder how to be New—but not in the old ways.

Question: I often feel the need to move quickly when I am distressed over something. What's wrong with wanting to get things cleared up in a hurry?

Answer: We must learn to live without the *immediate* if we wish Wonder to show us the *complete*.

Question: When I look at a tree, a computer, or a coffee maker, my mind grasps what I am seeing the very instant I see it. There is no delay between what my eyes behold and the arrival of its understanding. But, when I look at some spiritual principles, like these dealing with Wonder, there is a definite delay in the arrival of my understanding—if it comes at all! What is this delay? Can you please help me understand the problem?

Answer: Yes. And you have asked an important question. It addresses the root of why we must learn to suspend our familiar answers and then learn how to wait for Wonder to bring us its Higher Insights. The gap between what we know and what we need to know to be strong and happy cannot be spanned with our present understanding. You must try and see this. If it could, *there would be no gap.* Our present understanding would already have us happy. So, we cannot build a bridge to the Wonderful world above us with our own thinking. Thought cannot not reach above itself.

Question: Then how will we ever reach this new understanding?

Answer: You must let it come to you.

Question: But how do I know it will? And how does Wisdom know when we are ready?

Answer: What is True knows you are ready to be shown real solutions when YOU know you can no longer show yourself the way. This unthinkable revelation is both the need and the invitation for real Wisdom to establish contact. Wondering is our part of building this bridge to Beyond, but only the Truth can complete it. Then, and only then, does the necessary understanding flow down into us in the form of insight.

Question: What if some people don't have the strength it takes to suspend their own solutions? How will they succeed if they can't hold out long enough for this new need to awaken their Wonder?

Answer: The only thing Truth asks of us is that we place it before all else. Where we all make a mistake is we think we know what it means to succeed! We do not know. We can't know. It is not our job to succeed. Our task is to *need* more light, *not to create it*. If we will do our part, the Truth will take care of the rest.

Question: How can just some new Insight give me the strength I need to keep myself from being weak? Understanding is necessary, but don't we need more than that to be strong?

Answer: Let's take first things first. Only higher insight can show you that weakness or sadness never really belonged to you in the first place.

Question: Now that's different! Who does it belong to if not me?

Answer: Weakness doesn't belong to anyone. All self suffering states arise from our unconscious identification with mistaken beliefs and mental notions about who we are and what we need to be happy.

Question: Can you give me an example of one of these mental errors; something I can sink my teeth into? I really would like to understand what you are getting at here.

Answer: All of us think in order to be happy and free we need wealth, position, or the approval of others. This unquestioned and self imposed mental mistake keeps us chained to selling ourselves and trying in vain to please others. What we really need to do is let go of these chains, not have them gold plated. Insight shows us the Truth of our situation and seeing the Truth of it sets us free.

Question: I want to get started right away with putting Wonder to work in my life. Where do I begin?

Answer: Working with Wonder always begins with self watchfulness; with staying awake to our own mental and emotional movements. This is not difficult and doesn't require any special abilities. Wondering is a natural expression of our True Nature, so it doesn't have to be created or drummed up. We need only allow Wonder to surface. Once we become conscious of its friendly forces—and permit them to dwell within our day to day awareness—they will flourish effortlessly.

Question: Should we try and concentrate our Wondering on any particular area of our life?

Answer: Awakening Wonder begins with becoming conscious of any one of those particular thoughts, feelings or events in your life which are unusual, repetitive, fearful or painful, intriguing or mysterious. Wonder will set the course if you will raise the sail of attention. For instance, the wish to understand an always aching heart, or bruised feelings, or why nervousness never ends—any of these self noticings serve as a fine beginning. But, the key to lasting success—no matter what subject of Wonder captures your attention—is for you to be willing to remain without your own conclusions. Remember, we need insight to teach us the lesson in our pain—and *not* to let that pain tell us, once again, who it is in our life that needs to be taught a lesson!

Question: Must Wonder be limited to ourself? What about other people and their problems? Can't we gain insights from the mistakes of others?

Answer: Generally not. It is far more profitable to notice how much we do wonder about others, and then let ourselves Wonder why we are so interested in someone else's difficulty. If we are willing, Wonder will reveal why we have this strange preference that turns out to be a self punishment! One of the great rewards that surface with this new kind of Higher Self Discovery is as we gain increased insight into our own previously unconscious inner conflicts, we also begin to understand everyone else's. This new knowledge is not only perfect protection, but it encourages us to keep our Wondering at home where it will do the most good.

Question: I often enjoy Wondering about the heavens and about all of the unknowns in this life. So much goes unexplained. What about these Wonders all around us? Aren't they worth our attention?

Answer: Yes, of course. Let Wonder lead you where it will. But we are all well advised to consider that there is no REAL Need on our part to Wonder about many of the questions that find their way into our mind. Much valuable time and energy—Higher Resources that could be put to work mining priceless insights—is spent foolishly seeking answers that serve no purpose other than to keep us distracted. Everything we need to know about this life and its sublime mysteries is contained right within our own True Nature. We needn't look any further. And this is the Wonder of it all.

Without going out of doors, one may know the whole world; without looking out of the window, one may see the Way of Heaven. The further one travels, the less one may know. Thus it is without moving you may know; without looking you shall see; without doing you shall succeed.

—Lao-tse

Chapter 6

How To Use The Wonders
In This Book

The Wonders you will meet in this book have been carefully crafted and specially shaped into the form of Higher self questions.

Each of these Wonder-based questions is designed to awaken within you not only the need for a new and healing answer, but to instantly reveal as well that your present mind will *not* be able to find it!

Don't be too concerned at this temporary and necessary impasse. As you will discover if you'll persist with your inner work, being placed between this spiritual rock and a hard place is all part of the Wonder of this book. So go ahead and allow yourself to be delivered before this window of Wonder. Stand there willingly with no thought for how the questions raised by your mind will be resolved. That part of this new and higher Wonderful process is not your responsibility.

Always remember the real healing insights we need in order to grow beyond ourselves are received and not self conceived. Treasure this last vital fact. In the years to come, it will help you detect the difference between inner riches and shiny rocks.

I know this hands-off approach to self enrichment seems unusual, but, nevertheless, don't be afraid to step back from yourself each time you step up to the window of Wonder. If you will permit Wonder-born forces to reveal you to yourself, you will discover that this kind of self seeing is the same as self solving; and that happily, self solving is one and the same as self freedom.

The following **Eight Ways To Add Power To Your Wonder** will help you turn the Wonders of this book into new strengths.

The First Way
Allow Your Need For Wonder To Grow

The clearer we can see the Truth of the fact that *how* we feel in life is directly connected to *what* we want *from* it, the greater will grow our need to Wonder what we have really been asking for.

1. Truth is never so close as when you want what is true more than you want what is you.

2. Let every moment show you what it is you treasure and then permit yourself to Wonder why you want to cling to that.

3. We must leave the familiar world *before* we can enter Wonder's world.

The Second Way
Follow Wonder Wherever It Needs To Go

Your need to know is the wind in Wonder's sails. Let Wonder supply the course. You stay on deck and wait and watch. Never mind if the seas sometimes rage. Let them. These storms can't touch you—which is what Wonder wants you to see. This new kind of safety is where you've always wanted to be. Sail on!

1. Never believe that the limit of your present view is the limit of your possibility.

2. Permitting the course of your life to be set by what you fear to find is like saying you want to see the whole world just as soon as you can get it to fit in a box.

3. You must be willing to enter the disturbance if you want to get out of it.

The Third Way
Use Wonder To Reveal Yourself To Yourself

There is no substitute for self realization since the only danger any of us face is hidden in what we don't know about ourself. Self knowledge is self safety.

1. It is always Right to Wonder about what is wrong, but this doesn't mean we should ever dwell on or in some prevalent darkness.

2. Make the Wonderful discovery that you aren't who you *think* you are.

3. The problems we will not face, we can't erase.

The Fourth Way
Meet The World With Wonder

Meet every event with the wish to learn the lesson *in* it; not to take something *from* it. When we choose the Way of Wonder through life, instead of our wish to win over it, Real Victory is guaranteed. Here's why. Unlike our insistence that we must win—which is always tied to the unconscious fear of loss—the Way of Wonder is born out of Wisdom which can never lose since it is already everything.

1. Reaching out for only the kind of rescue you can recognize is like climbing into a hole and then throwing yourself a rope.

2. There is no such thing as a good reason to feel bad unless we unconsciously believe that feeling bad is the proof we want to feel good.

3. Meeting life with the pretense that we already know what it is all about keeps us from discovering what *we* are all about.

The Fifth Way
Place Wonder's Power To Reveal Before
Fear's Insistence To Conceal

Fear wants you to believe that if you can bury some self weakness out of sight—or explain it away—that this choice is the same as having it out of mind. Wonder wants you to *see* that the only weaknesses you ever have to live with are the ones fear has convinced you to hide. Now you choose whether it's better to reveal or conceal.

1. Discovering where you have been choosing against yourself is the same as finding the power you need to choose in favor of yourself.

2. Fearful thoughts and feelings can only tell you where not to look within yourself, and then convince you that living thus restricted is the only option available at the moment.

3. All fear-filled solutions are the concealed continuation of the thing feared—so now you know what *not* to do!

The Sixth Way
Always Boldly Wonder What Is Higher

Daring to live without conclusions is the same as learning to live without tragedy. This special kind of self suspension is not the avoidance of life; it is the one bold course through which is revealed, that in life, there is always something Higher.

1. The need to live the unlimited life is our first real contact with that which is Limitless.

2. Abandon all answers about what to do with recurring problems that don't change anything but themselves.

3. The Fact is everything changes—nothing stays the same—which means that every moment you can choose to Wonder Higher.

The Seventh Way
Give Up Your Way And Let Wonder Show You The Way

We never crash so hard or feel so lost as when we are certain of *our* direction—and then life decides to change *its* course. There is another way. Learning to want what life wants is the same as giving yourself everything life has to offer.

1. Fighting to take something from life and living in fear of life are inseparable.

2. Looking to self conceived notions for where to find self safety is like asking the captain of the Titanic which part of his ship has the most secure cabins.

3. THE Way is always there once you let go of your way.

The Eighth Way
Let Wonder Lead To Wonder

When Wonder-awakened insight delivers you to the base of a seemingly impassable inner mountain, don't confuse *what* you see for *who* you are. That's the wrong view and the wrong you. The Wonder of it all is just above your present position—and starting over is how you climb higher.

1. The real quality of our life is not determined by what we have won from it, but by what we have discovered within it.

2. Believing you can have insights without Wonder is like thinking you can climb without reaching.

3. Dare to Wonder what life would be like if you could get yourself out of the way, and then turn that Wonder loose.

Getting Started With The Wonder Of It All

The next six chapters are divided into six categories of Wonderings. Each of the six individual chapters has ten separate Wonders that relate directly to that chapter's heading. For instance, in Chapter 7, *The Wonder Of Being Me*, the first Wonder you'll meet is "The Wonder Of Finding The Way."

This Wonder—like all of the other 60 Wonders you're about to meet in the forthcoming pages—is meant to stir you in an indescribable manner. You'll know you've been touched—but you won't know by what. This is exactly the way it's intended to be. Give each and every one of these Wonders all the time *it* wants. Don't rush. These higher forms of truthful self questionings work best if we open ourselves to their secret promptings and then just let them grow as they will in our consciousness.

You see, real Wonder is a rare and special kind of spiritual seed. Our task isn't to make it flower, but to *allow it to reveal its fullness* in its own time. Then we enjoy it forever because the fragrance of that new and healing self understanding now belongs to us.

Following are a few Wondrous Ways to help you

go further with your important inner work.

1. Take any one of the Wonders from this book that you feel the strong need to work with and find some way to keep it before your consciousness as much and as often as possible.

2. Watch for any and all of the various expressions of your particular Wondering in your everyday activities and relationships.

3. Be sure and give yourself enough time for at least ten minutes of quiet Wondering in the morning and evening. Remember: This doesn't mean to sit there and *think*. Real Wonder is your heightened *awareness* of the need for a new answer while knowing at the same time that you must *not* answer that need from your old self.

4. Go ahead and give yourself permission to drift off to sleep each night in a state of Conscious Wonder.

5. Whatever else you may do, come to no conclusions of your own; let insights come to you.

Chapter 7

The Wonder Of Being Me

The Wonder Of Finding The Way

Just as a mother wouldn't call outside to her children to bid them come in from the cold— and then lock the front door so they couldn't enter—neither does the Truth invite you and me to find a Higher life and then deny us entrance to its Way. And this makes me Wonder ...

... If something blocks the way of our happiness, if we are somehow locked out of love, shouldn't we consider the possibility we're standing in the wrong place ... and knocking at the wrong door?

Add These Insights To Your Wonder About Finding The Way

1. When life brings you a weighted, bitter cup—instead of asking yourself—"why is this cup so heavy and its draft so sharp?"—learn to honestly ask your-self—"how did this cup find its way into my hand when no one could have made me pick it up?"

2. Never accept any condition which isn't to your perfect liking, for everything can change in that one moment when you do.

3. Frustration is not the proof we know the Way and that something just won't let us pass; the only thing the presence of frus-tration proves is that we'd rather live with our own insistence than see that *that* is the very thing standing in our Way.

> *Whilst a man seeks good ends, he is strong by the whole strength of nature ... The perception of this law of Laws awakens in the mind a sentiment which we call the religious sentiment, and which makes our highest happiness. Wonderful is its power to charm and to command. It is a mountain air.*
> —Ralph Waldo Emerson

The Wonder Of Self Newness

We are never quite so bored as when we know what to expect. Be it the plot of that movie we've seen more than once, or the predictable behavior of some particularly unpleasant person, there is a real and natural dread of having to go through what we've been through before. And this makes me Wonder ...

... Isn't it true that each time we name for ourself how we feel about something, this is exactly the same as taking ourself, once again, into emotional territory we've already been through and covered?

Add These Insights To Your Wonder About Self Newness

1. It's impossible to discover who you really are if you limit what you are willing to find out about yourself to only what you want to know.

2. Before we can enter into the presence of what is authentically new, we are first called to leave the safety of all that we have known.

3. Each daring dismissal of what we have already been is our conscious invitation to what we are yet to be.

Every man has within him a continent of undiscovered character. Happy is he who proves to be the Columbus of his Spirit.

—Johann W. von Goethe

The Wonder Of Insisting
On Unhappiness

When we stop to ask ourself why do we go through the daily strife that we do, we answer that the pursuit of our happiness demands some sacrifice. And so this is our sadness: *We endure what we must to achieve what we want.* And in this assumption we live with the unspoken certainty that to do otherwise would be to fall into the waiting hands of unhappiness. And this makes me Wonder ...

... Is unhappiness really a power unto itself, a force to be dealt with on a daily basis, or is its only authority over us measured by how much of it we think we must tolerate within ourself in order to make ourself happy?

Add These Insights To Your Wonder About Insisting On Unhappiness

1. Unhappiness is unnatural.

2. When sad about something, we must work to see the connection between what we *want* and how we *feel*—so that one day we'll no longer go along with *wanting* to *feel* unhappy.

3. Effortless happiness arises as unconscious insistence subsides.

Hardly a man, whatever his circumstances and situation, but if you get his confidence, will tell you that he is not happy. It is however certain that all men are not unhappy in the same degree, though by these accounts we might almost be tempted to think so. Is not this to be accounted for, but supposing that all men measure the happiness they possess by the happiness they desire, or think they deserve.

—Lord Greville

The Wonder Of Free Will And Choice

Even when trying physical circumstances prevent us from doing what we'd rather, we're *always* free to do what we will in the invisible world of our thoughts and feelings. In this inner realm, *what we think* and *how we feel* is ours alone to command. Here we can embrace what we treasure most—and our interior life is a perfectly reliable reflection—a moment by moment experience of what it is we *really* want. And this makes me Wonder ...

... What if suffering is something we've been doing *to ourselves* because somehow, somewhere down the line, we forgot that any time we want, we can choose *not* to feel bad?

Add These Insights To Your Wonder About Free Will And Choice

1. Once you know what it means to choose in favor of yourself, there is no power in the universe that can make you choose against yourself.

2. Life can't make us walk in any direction if our feet don't already point that way.

3. Make it clearer and clearer to yourself that what you *want* is to *make what you want* clearer and clearer to yourself!

No action will be considered blameless, unless the will was so, for by the will the act was dictated.

—Seneca A Lucius

The Wonder Of Self Possession

I know a man and a woman who have
worked hard to overcome challenging circumstances. They have possessions and position. You can see the certainty in his stride
and the pride in her eyes. But, I have also
seen this woman when she was unable to
smile and when—for all of his conquests—
this man was convinced he had nothing;
when both were temporarily sure, beyond
the shadow of a doubt, that all was in vain.
Who is this man and woman? Don't you recognize them? And this makes me Wonder ...

... What have we really gained for all we
think we possess if these sorely earned victo-
ries can be put asunder by the merest of
thoughts that visit us with defeat?

Add These Insights to Your Wonder About Self Possession

1. Real self possession begins with the understanding that the thought which says, "I own this" or "I own that" doesn't even own itself!

2. Only that person who possesses his or her own mind does not feel the pain of being dispossessed when that same mind is suddenly *made* to accept change or decides to change *itself*.

3. Real security isn't in what you possess, but it is within what you are.

> *Self-government is, indeed, the noblest rule on earth; the object of a loftier ambition than the possession of crowns or scepters. The monarch of his own mind is the only real potentate.*
>
> —John Caird

The Wonder Of Inner Healing

Have you ever noticed how the body heals itself? The process seems so simple, yet so extraordinary. When something heals, it is re-unified. It comes back together. In this way, a hurting hand becomes whole and healthy again. It mends. But what about a heavy, aching heart—or that unresolved resentment or sorrow? Here too our pain is a sign that somewhere *within* we are apart— that something divides us; and because this inner state of self compromise lingers on un-detected, we're denied the spiritual well-being that must attend self healing. And this makes me Wonder ...

... How can we ever hope to heal *in ourself* what we aren't willing to reveal *to ourself*— for isn't self revealing what we need for In-ner-Healing?

Add These Insights to Your Wonder About Inner Healing

1. Never believe any thought or feeling that pushes you apart can ever be one that will pull you together.

2. We may discover ourself—or defend it— but never succeed at either, should we foolishly choose the latter.

3. Nothing can come between you and full Inner Healing except the inner lie that you are already healed.

> *Never let us be discouraged with our-*
> *selves. It is not when we are conscious*
> *of our faults that we are most wicked;*
> *on the contrary, we are less so. We see*
> *by a brighter light; and let us remember*
> *for our comfort that we never perceive*
> *our sins till we begin to cure them.*
> —Francis Fenelon

The Wonder Of Pleasure And Desire

We have all owned the object of at least one of our longings, but we've never been able to hold onto the pleasant feelings it stirred within us. Pleasure cannot be possessed. Desire is that exciting, hypnotic inner-state, wherein we can't remember that the present pleasure we pursue is the *same* pleasure we couldn't hold onto the last time around. The pleasure pursued always fails to deliver our expectation because the sweet sensation we strain to collect isn't real. It's only a memory; a phantom projection of some past pleasure; an alluring thought-form cast up into our consciousness as an image that first tempts and then hungers for itself. And this makes me Wonder ...

... If the more we attempt to capture some pleasure, the more we become its captive— where is the pleasure in that?

Add These Insights To Your Wonder About Pleasure And Desire

1. Running after pleasure is like trying to capture a beautiful echo in a butterfly net.

2. No desire can ever remember that the pleasure it desires is powerless to satisfy itself.

3. It's only when we *stop* trying to please ourself that we start to discover the natural pleasure of our own Being.

> *The man of pleasure little knows the perfect joy he loses for the disappointing gratifications which he pursues.*
> —Joseph Addison

The Wonder Of A Fixed Point Of View

When we were small, there was little in our life that was hard except for the way in which we played. Those seem brighter days somehow. Less troubled. The only time the idea of position ever entered into our young mind was when it came time to take part in some game on the playground. Try to remember. Back then it didn't matter where you stood because fun was fun from *any* point of view. And this makes me Wonder ...

... Is it really life that's grown harder—or is it that now we live from a fixed point of view—which only makes it feel that way?

Add These Insights To Your Wonder About A Fixed Point of View

1. Whenever Life seems too heavy to bear, remember all you're really carrying around is the misplaced certainty that you have to hold onto some punishing image or idea.

2. Anger is our ignorant insistence that what doesn't work should.

3. To be open doesn't mean to be shallow; nor is what can bend always weak; consider the ocean and the oak.

It is within our power to have no opinion about a thing, and not to be disturbed in our soul, for things themselves have no natural power to form our judgements.

—Marcus Aurelius

The Wonder Of Individuality

The more we search in another's eye for a glimpse of ourself, the more we fear even their briefest blink. What greater contradiction and source of constant uncertainty can there be than seeking to have our own sense of individuality confirmed by others? And this makes me Wonder ...

... Wouldn't the true individual be that one person who, rather than seeking his sense of self in the approval of the crowd, quietly realizes that nothing a thousand crowds can confer has any power to make him more than he already *is*?

Add These Insights to Your Wonder About Individuality

1. Permanent individuality is the gift of Spirit that comes only to those who are willing to see they have no real life of their own.

2. The common mind succumbs to its sufferings, but the individual one sees it has nothing in common with worthless states.

3. Authentic individuality includes an abiding compassion born out of the personal discovery that who you really are is both a part of—and apart from—everyone you see.

Each individual nature has its own beauty. In every company, at every fireside, one is struck with the riches of nature, when he hears so many tones, all musical, sees in each person original manners which have a proper and peculiar charm, and reads new expression of face. He perceives that nature has laid for each the foundations of a divine building if the soul will build thereon.

—Ralph Waldo Emerson

The Wonder Of Self Image

All expectations of how others should see us are based on how we secretly see ourself. These moving mental pictures, called self images, are highly valued—and considered a measure of our self esteem. But they are really the measure of our misery. Let's look at the evidence. Have you ever noticed the outrage and anger arising from within whenever someone treats you in such a way that it's clear they don't see you the way you do? Of course the rationale behind our ensuing self destructive indignation is that we're not going to let anyone treat us badly. And this makes me Wonder ...

... Is there anyone who treats himself worse than that image-laden person who knows how he should or shouldn't be treated?

Add These Insights To Your Wonder About Self Image

1. The secret and severe punishment of any self image is that all images must be perpetually maintained for fear they'll fade away.

2. There is no natural need to think about yourself at all.

3. It's only when we dare to stop self creating that we can realize we've already been created with everything we'll ever need to be complete.

Prize not thyself by what thou has, but by what thou art; he that values a jewel by its golden frame, or a book by its silver clasps, or a man by his vast estate, errs.

—Francis Quarles

Let Your Wonder Grow About Yourself With These Ten Truths

1. Your nature is your life's request.

2. Real freedom is the capacity to act from intelligence, not the ability to create an explanation for your choices.

3. Nothing imprisons a person more than his own self constructed steel-like certainty that he must learn to live with defeat.

4. Criticizing someone is not the proof that you can do it better.

5. The Truth will speak to you when you no longer have anything left to talk to yourself about.

6. Unless "other" correction begins with self correction, it's just self deception.

7. Self certainty is self enclosure.

8. Who "I am" in this moment is what the next moment will be.

9. If we have pain it's because we keep insisting that what we *want* is what we *need*.

10. It's only when we stop trying to live up to our best idea of who we should be that we finally glimpse it wasn't our *idea* in the first place—and then we can get on to the real business of discovering who we *really* are.

Chapter 8

The Wonder Of Relationship

The Wonder Of Keeping
Timeless Company

We all know that a kite belongs in the company of the open sky. When you put the nature of a kite together with the nature of the wind, something Wonderful happens. The two are meant for one another. Their union brings an immediate expectation of effortless new heights. That they belong together is obvious. And this unspoken understanding of their special relationship makes it all the clearer that a kite, without the company of the wind, is only half of what it is intended to be. And this makes me Wonder ...

... Just like the kite without the wind, are not we too only half of what we're intended to be when we aren't in the company of that which is Timeless?

Add These Insights To Your Wonder About Keeping Timeless Company

1. Anytime we choose we can stop meeting life from that lower nature which always wants something—and enter into a new kind of relationship with life from our True Nature—which already knows it *is* everything.

2. Inwardly and outwardly, it is better to be alone than to keep bad company.

3. When you do your best to choose the company of what is Truly Timeless, this Sovereign State will, in turn, choose you.

> *What is companionship where nothing that improves the intellect is communicated, and where the larger heart contracts itself to the model and dimension of the smaller.*
>
> —Walter S. Landor

The Wonder Of Weakness

If only we could look deeply enough into the flashing eyes of that angry person, we would see someone before us who is just plain scared. And looking even deeper still, we could see someone secretly shaking from fear of losing control—and someone who, for that moment—doesn't know what else to do but to try and ACT strong so as to not reveal the weakness that is now carrying him along. And this makes me Wonder ...

... What would happen if we refused to ever again tremble or flee before the tempest of anyone's WEAKNESS—including our own?

Add These Insights To Your Wonder About Weakness

1. What you have once conquered within yourself is forever conquered wherever and in whomever you have occasion to meet it again.

2. The weakness we will consciously endure is but the seed of a new and enduring strength.

3. Where is the need to be delivered from any enemy whose only strength is my belief in weakness?

It is good to know; it is better to do; it is best to BE. To be pure and strong, to be honest and earnest, to be kindly and thoughtful, and in all to be True, to be manly and womanly. He can do more for others who has done most with himself.

—Samuel D. Gordon

The Wonder Of The Enemy

After we make an enemy, we tend to think of that individual as being entirely irritating. But, generally speaking, what really turns us against these people is usually just ONE particularly disturbing mannerism or characteristic of theirs that rubs us the wrong way. And yet, it's impossible to rail against some invisible condition in another without having first discovered it within ourself—else how could we be so painfully conscious of and aggravated by its presence? And this makes me Wonder . . .

. . . Perhaps the only real enemy is within what I don't want to know about myself?

Add These Insights To Your Wonder About The Enemy

1. The inherent problem with trying to avoid those who don't like us lies in the fact that the only condition we ever encounter is our own nature.

2. When it comes to a conflict with another we can either learn what is true or go on defending what is false—but this choice should be self evident: What is True needs no defense and what is false can't be defended.

3. To cancel all painful self concern over what some embittered person may be thinking about you—just remember that no one can think about another without first thinking about him or herself—so no one is ever really thinking about you at all!

Did a person but know the value of an enemy, he would purchase him with gold.

—Raunci

The Wonder Of Love And Self Sacrifice

Consider the logic: Before we can ever give someone something of our own, we must first take it from ourself. Otherwise, what's in the giving? This concept is easy to grasp when it comes to food or money. But what is that we take from ourself when we want to give our love? What is it that's really ours to give? And this makes me Wonder ...

... Is love an essence we possess, some quality or quantity to be bestowed on another— or is love the quiet willingness to bear ourself; the conscious, self sacrifice contained in our refusal to add even the smallest measure of our own suffering onto the shoulders of another?

Add These Insights To Your Wonder About Love And Self Sacrifice

1. The cost of love is the measure of ourself that we must give up to buy it.

2. Not hurting the one who has hurt you is love in action.

3. Perhaps the greatest mystery concerning the Grace of God's love is that it never mingles with what is already draft, but flows only into an empty cup.

We never know how much one loves until we know how much he or she is willing to endure and suffer for us; and it is the suffering element that measures love—To hold our nature in the willing service of another, is the Divine idea of the human character.

—H. W. Beecher

The Wonder Of Self Protection

Avoiding relationships may place us outside the danger of those who would betray us—but this same action presses us into an unseen, ongoing relationship with our own fear of being hurt. Within this alliance with weakness, we become the unwitting captive of our own impossible wish to be psychologically safe—because having first embraced the fear of being hurt—there's just no question now that we need to protect ourself. So, we begin to isolate our heart. And that's the way it goes—one piece at a time—until we lose contact with the one part of ourself that gives life its beauty and meaning. And this makes me Wonder ...

... How far does weakness have to go before it begins to see that it's doing to itself the very thing it claims to fear?

Add These Insights To Your Wonder About Self Protection

1. The willingness to go ahead and risk being hurt is the same as being willing to learn how to stop hurting.

2. We would never again have to exclaim that no one will ever make us feel "that way" again if—right at the moment of our declaration—we would inwardly see that the *only* thing making us feel "that way" right then was our wish *not* to feel that way!

3. The nature that renews itself needs no protection, and your True Nature is newness itself.

> *There is great beauty in going through life without anxiety or fear. Half our fears are baseless, and the other half discreditable.*
> —Christian Bovee

The Wonder Of Self Love

Self love is incapable of considering others. It only thinks it thinks of others. All it's really concerned with is what others are thinking about it. And the only feeling self love cares for is its own feeling that it really cares—otherwise, it doesn't care at all—as evidenced by how it treats those who it thinks have stopped caring about it. And this makes me Wonder ...

... Is self love really love at all?

Add These Insights To Your Wonder About Self Love

1. Self love never sees itself as wrong; and it's only out of the goodness of its own perfected patience that it can tolerate so much imperfection in others.

2. Self love measures everyone else by its own index of excellence, wherein all who are judged not only fall somewhat short, but the judge is always made that much taller.

3. Since the root of self love is self reference, whose very nature *separates* itself from all that it sees, then what else is self love other than the ultimate self isolation?

Self love is the most delicate and most tenacious of our sentiments; a mere nothing will wound it but nothing can kill it. The shadow of the sun is largest when its beams are lowest. On the contrary, we are always least when we make ourselves the greatest.

—Villefre

The Wonder Of Compassion

Real compassion lies within our ability to remember that an angry, vengeful, or hate-
filled person is usually just someone who can
no longer bear the weary weight of his or her
own carefully concealed despair. And the
aching has to be unloaded somewhere. She's
secretly worried sick you've stopped caring,
so she lashes out. He's afraid you don't take
him seriously, so he's driven to respond in
sarcasm or disrespect. And this makes me
Wonder ...

... Would any of us be so quick in wanting to
punish those who claw at us—if we could
but see that their own pain is already more
than punishment enough?

Add These Insights To Your Wonder About Compassion

1. There are always some people who want to pull you into their pain, but it is highly compassionate to refuse being taken in.

2. Our capacity for compassion is in direct proportion to our willingness to consciously suffer.

3. Compassion is its own reward—for to help another over any hurdle is to secretly lift yourself.

> *If we could read the secret history of our enemies, we should find in each man's life sorrow and suffering enough to disarm all hostility.*
> —Henry Wadsworth Longfellow

The Wonder Of Resentment

There is no such thing as right resentment. Each one of these burning, inner irritations is born out of our refusal to be self ruling. Saying "yes" when we really want to say "no" is just one good example. Fawning before others for fear of their reprisal is another. Both weak actions breed self wrecking resentment because our wish to be falsely accommodating compromises our natural need for self command. And this makes me Wonder ...

... Why are we more concerned with how others feel about us than we are with how we're making ourself feel?

Add These Insights To Your Wonder About Resentment

1. Resentment burns up the resenter long before the one resented even notices the flame.

2. The reason we seldom forgive those whom we resent isn't that they may not have had a change of heart, but because if we even suspected they had, we'd have to let go of our hatred, and that would change us.

3. It's a waste of time to resent some person or group for their seeming authority over you—when that same energy can be used to see *you* gave them that power—and what you've given is always yours to take back.

We are never more discontented with others than when we are discontented with ourselves. The consciousness of wrongdoing makes us irritable, and our heart in its cunning quarrels with what is outside it, in order that it may deafen the clamor within.

—Henri Amiel

The Wonder Of Seeking Approval

Seeking and receiving approval from others is like sitting down hungry to an imaginary meal. You're invited to eat all you want, but no matter how much fantasy food is served or how well presented, you can never get your fill. Your hunger remains. And so this much is clear: No fictional feast can ever satisfy our need for nourishment. But this fact isn't so apparent when it comes to our appetite for approval. We still look to others for some sense of ourself even though the very moment it's received, it must be renewed. And this makes me Wonder ...

... What good is any feeling we may have about ourself if it only lasts as long as others agree to it?

Add These Insights To Your Wonder About Seeking Approval

1. Believing you can't be happy without the approval of others is like thinking that you can't see beauty without someone else's eyes.

2. Ask yourself what profit is there in the praise of the thousands who condemn themselves a hundred times a day?

3. If you want something truly Lasting in this life, you must not seek it within any world you presently know.

> *Consider what your bondage is in the world. What do you not have to suffer to keep the esteem of those men whom you scorn?*
>
> —Francis Fenelon

The Wonder Of Empty Apologies

Anyone can be sorry. And then be sorry again ... and again. This is the state of our personal affairs—where all that ever changes is what we have to apologize about. So it would seem our sorrow runs shallow. To go beyond our own empty apologies takes special inner work. Real Sorrow— which leads to individual harmlessness— arises not from some passing regret over what we've done but out of meeting that side of our nature which parents dark deeds. Just to say, "I'm sorry" for this or that, without being conscious of what it is within us that's against us and others, guarantees we will only stay sorry. And this makes me Wonder ...

... Are we really sorry when we're cruel to others, or are we only sorry for what we fear that cruelty may have cost us?

Add These Insights To Your Wonder About Empty Apologies

1. It is a kind act and highly intelligent to return all empty apologies unopened.

2. When we are really sorry we can no longer be driven to think about ourself—for we know it was out of rampant self centeredness that came the harm in the first place.

3. Only when we stop making our own empty apologies will we never again be fooled by anyone else's.

> *The path of sorrow, and that path alone, leads to the land where sorrow is unknown; no traveller ever reached that blessed abode who found not thorns and briars in his road.*
>
> —William Cowper

Ten Important Points To Ponder About
The Wonder Of Relationships

1. When your intentions are clear, it doesn't matter what anyone else's are.

2. You wouldn't buy an empty box from a tricky vendor, so why buy an apology with nothing in it from a repeat offender.

3. Trying to find goodness in the lesser of two evils is like looking for a rainbow in the rear of a cave.

4. Conscious self awareness is to correct choice what good directions are to certain arrival.

5. All judgement of others is born out of our own uncertainty.

6. You are not responsible for any other human being's hatred of life.

7. Always remember the person you're speaking to hears your inner state first and then the words you are saying.

8. Most people would rather spend their energy resenting the fruits of another man's orchard than go to work and quietly grow their own.

9. Keep your distance from people who are always sorry, or you'll be.

10. We never stand so small as when we leap upon the back of another's weakness to give ourselves the feeling of being tall.

Chapter 9

The Wonder Of Fear, Frustration And Other Worries

The Wonder Of Fear And Ignorance

The dark giants of fear and ignorance are closely allied. The True slayer of these evil giants is the one who knows what is in his or her power and what isn't. For instance, it's within no one's power to slay fear, because *fear exists only as a shadow of the unknown*— and shadows can't be slain. But, it is within our power to challenge and conquer *what is unknown* since *nothing* can prevent us from learning. This is the One Sword that shatters all dark shadows—for when the one giant falls, can the other but follow? And this makes me Wonder ...

... If we find ourselves living in the shadow of any fear, isn't that the same as saying that we have unconsciously agreed to live with ignorance?

Add These Insights To Your Wonder About Fear And Ignorance

1. Giving yourself permission to know that you don't know is the same as giving yourself the opportunity to learn.

2. The unknown is really just our own uninvestigated mind which looks out upon and then sees each new footpath in its own image.

3. Moment by moment—one Wonder-filled step at a time—you can choose to consciously enter into and dismantle what is yet unknown—and when at last it topples, where is there for fear to hide?

Ignorance is the night of the mind, but a night without moon or stars.

—Confucius

The Wonder Of Anxiety

Here's an interesting and observable fact. All negative emotions contradict themselves. They promise their possessor one thing, but deliver its opposite. Consider anxiety. This state always claims to know that *something must be done right away* in order to secure some potential or developing emergency. But, the *more* power we give to *it*, the *less* power we have over ourself to stop our own growing feelings of insecurity. And this makes me Wonder . . .

. . . What good is there in trying to avert any future worry if—as a result of that futile attempt—we unknowingly create the very sorrow we had thought to avoid?

Add These Insights To Your Wonder About Anxiety

1. Start suspecting that those anxious thoughts and feelings you catch trying to sell you an umbrella are not there to shelter you from some *approaching* storm ... but that their sole purpose is to lure you into one.

2. A mind awakened to itself is free of all painful contradictions.

3. Anxiety is not the natural condition attending our heart's wish to ever expand itself, but rather anxiety is an unnatural state which always accompanies our certainty that we already *know* what we need to achieve that aim.

> *When we are unhurried and wise, we perceive that only great and worthy things have any permanent and absolute existence, that petty fears and petty pleasures are but the shadow of reality. This is always exhilarating and sublime.*
>
> —Henry David Thoreau

The Wonder Of Useless Feelings

We've always believed that what we feel, *the way we feel*, is born out of what we *see* unfolding before our eyes. But, we can easily prove that what we think we are seeing is actually based on whatever our dominant feeling is at that moment. A simple illustration is worth a thousand words: Even though the sun may be shining, who do we know that sees a bright day when he or she is feeling down or defeated? And this makes me Wonder ...

... Why is it so hard sometimes to see that the only thing even remotely useless about life are those feelings that say it's so?

Add These Insights To Your Wonder About Useless Feelings

1. Any thought or feeling that wants you to feel badly over anything is useless.

2. One fail-safe test to find out if some inner condition is useless or not is to quietly determine that starting right now, you're going to live without it; if fear follows, then you know for sure.

3. The true measure of our life isn't the kind of events we're given to meet, but what kind of person *we are* when we meet them.

> *It is in our power to have no opinion about a thing, and not to be disturbed in our soul, for things have no natural power to form our judgement.*
> —Marcus Aurelius

The Wonder Of Self Awakening

We have almost no choice when nightmares come but to let all of these unwanted forces and forms locked within our unconscious mind run their course. We awaken when we can no longer bear the dream; when it's simply too painful for us to remain asleep. Once our eyes are open, there's great relief in discovering they had only been closed, and our problem was just that we'd been locked in the dark theater of our own mind without knowing it. Once awakened and conscious of our true condition outside the scary scenes within, our fears naturally vanish by themselves. That's what it means to wake up. That's part of it's sweetness. And this makes me Wonder ...

... Shouldn't the grim spectre of any fear in our *waking* life cause us to consider that we may be yet still sleeping?

Add These Insights To Your Wonder About Self Awakening

1. The difference between being awake to yourself and being asleep in yourself is the difference between being the wind or just a leaf in it.

2. When our wish to awaken is greater than our desire to keep dreaming, every event will serve our continued awakening instead of keeping us unwitting servants of our dreams.

3. Before we can awaken *to* our Self, we must first awaken *from* ourself.

Nothing is more hidden from us than the illusion which lives with us day by day, and our greatest illusion is to believe that we are who we think ourselves to be.

—Henri Amiel

The Wonder Of Finding Freedom

If we look for something outside of ourself to give us freedom, our search must always leave us empty handed—for nothing imprisons us other than our own unawakened nature. The few who are free are those who have found that freedom isn't won on some distant shore. It's not there. No condition gives it rise. *Free is what we are* each time we can catch ourself about to build some prison out of thought—because our awakened consciousness instantly cancels our imagined captivity. And as our self created agony fades, so does the desperate need to escape. We are already free. And this makes me Wonder ...

... Who are more hopelessly enslaved than those who imagine themselves to be free?

Add These Insights To Your Wonder About Finding Freedom

1. To free yourself of any dark feeling that dominates you, just remember you are free to lose interest in its torment any time *you* want.

2. Most men and women never find freedom because they're so busy looking for an open door somewhere that they never notice the ladder awaiting them right at their feet.

3. Don't be afraid to admit to yourself that you don't know anything about freedom, and then watch how this confession frees you to begin finding your way out.

He is the freeman whom the Truth makes free, and all are slaves beside.
—William Cowper

The Wonder Of Problems

There is no such thing as a problem. None really exist. Permit yourself to see the truth of this by following these facts: Issues we understand aren't problems. Issues we don't, are. This shows us that the only real problem we ever face is just our own lack of understanding. But even this condition can't be called a problem, because the only limitations governing our ability to grow in understanding are found in our own fixed assumptions that we already know all there is to know. And this makes me Wonder ...

... If a problem seems to persist, wouldn't it be wise to view our present way of thinking as part of that problem, instead of searching it for the solution?

Add These Insights To Your Wonder About Problems

1. Problems have no real authority over your real nature, just as darkness has no power over light.

2. The joy in encountering something greater than our present understanding is that within our persistent wish to understand it, we're required to reveal to ourself certain beliefs once held in unconscious certainty; unquestioned beliefs which—once released—show themselves to be the only problem we ever really had.

3. When met with the wish to learn, problems soon become self powers you've yet to discover within yourself.

No truth so sublime but it may be trivial tomorrow in the light of new thoughts. People wish to be settled; only as far as they are unsettled is there any hope for them.

—Ralph Waldo Emerson

The Wonder Of Painful Patterns

Routines are important for order. Order gives rise to security. Security is the backbone of freedom. And from freedom comes the power of self command to choose as we please. But it often happens that in our search for this freedom we turn into captives of routine; where our fear to stray outside of what is familiar becomes stronger than our original wish to be free. And within this restricted circle of self there is no longer any choice. We cease to rule our own day. And this makes me Wonder ...

... At what point do patterns turn into prisons without walls?

Add These Insights To Your Wonder About Painful Patterns

1. Quietly make it clear to yourself that there's no other end to painful patterns besides just ending them—and then get on with it.

2. At the foundation of every painful pattern is an unconscious trade-off where it's decided that in return for knowing what's about to happen to us, we'll agree to repeat what makes us unhappy.

3. Remember when working to break free of any pattern, that the inner place where you meet the most resistance isn't as far as you can go—*it's just as far as you know ...* for now.

> *What a curious phenomena it is that you can get men to die for the liberty of the world who will not make the little sacrifice that is needed to free themselves from their own individual bondage.*
>
> —Bruce Barton

The Wonder Of Attachments

The pleasure we take from something we know doesn't belong to us is different from the feelings we have about those things we consider ours. Having to give up something of ours often hurts. Saying goodbye to someone else's possession poses no problem. There's no attachment. But Life itself belongs to neither friend nor personal account. In life everything changes; nothing can be truly owned. After all, the would-be owners don't even own themselves—let alone what they would hold in their hands or heart. And this makes me Wonder ...

... How would we feel towards that person or cherished possession in *this* moment—if we knew beyond a shadow of a doubt—that in some *next moment*—things must change?

Add These Insights To Your Wonder About Attachments

1. When we can see beauty in the *arrival* of a thing, as well as in the thing itself, then when at last its time of *departure* appears, we may—and well might—see the beauty in that.

2. All we're really attached to is a feeling of ourself which—even when it tears at us—we still won't release.

3. Let yourself wonder whether it's possible to embrace something fully without ever picking it up.

Remember the wheel of Providence is
always in motion; and the spoke that is
uppermost will be under; and therefore
mix trembling always with your joy.
—Philip Henry

The Wonder Of Frustrated Wants

We want to be happy and there's nothing wrong in that. We want the world we live in—whatever its fabric and size—to first recognize, and then somehow help us, to celebrate that unique sense of our own being that's ours alone to express. We want to feel worthwhile—and know that others feel that way about us too. And we want life to confirm our purpose; to make clear the way for who we're yet to become. We just want things to go the way we want them to go. But sometimes they just don't. And when this happens, we not only lose sight of that better life we seek, but even the life we have seems to turn bitter. And this makes me Wonder . . .

. . . What's the good of any *want* if part of its power is to spoil what we already have?

Add These Insights To Your Wonder About Frustrated Wants

1. When any feeling of frustration arises, it can and should be used to re-awaken our need for renewing our aim to want what life wants.

2. Freedom from haunting wants arrives in proportion to our willingness to see that the wanter within is a dark and bottomless basket.

3. The moth flies frustrated into the flame and falling cries out...
   the light's to blame.

Everyone is poorer in proportion as he has more wants, and counts not what he has, but wishes only for what he has not.

—Manilius

The Wonder Of Loneliness

Fear, anger and pretense are the terrible trio. These three tormentors always walk in line, one behind the other. Challenge fear and see how quickly anger supports it with its flashing strength. Challenge anger and watch how pretense jumps to its defense, protesting that *you* were the one who made it take the offensive. But challenge pretense and it reveals itself as being full of fear. It's afraid of being alone and all it can do is pretend that it's not. And this makes me Wonder ...

... Is there anything standing behind loneliness?

Add These Insights To Your Wonder About Loneliness

1. Loneliness is the opportunity to be alone—and being consciously alone is the only way you'll ever learn to see through the lie of loneliness.

2. The next time loneliness pierces your heart, let yourself wonder if you'd feel that way without the company of all those dark thoughts telling you how lonely you are.

3. Who you really are would no more look for itself in a lonely feeling than you would go searching for sunbeams at the bottom of a cave.

Alone, man—weak, tottering—yet with God this handful of dust made to be unmade, molded to be molding, grasps the ungraspable, utters the ineffable, and when what seems too profound for human intelligence sweeps into the horizon, solitude is no more and misery has departed.

—Emil G. Hirsch

A Short Summary To Help Wonder Fears
And Worries Away

1. You don't own crashing emotions any more than you own a storm you walk through.

2. Ask a question in terror and you will always receive a terrifying answer.

3. What wants you to feel useless won't be happy until it uses you up.

4. Thinking about how to protect yourself in the future is like standing on your own toe so that you'll know how to feel—should someone be so rude as to step on it later.

5. Fear needs your cooperation to frighten you.

6. To have your own life doesn't mean you're in charge of what happens around you, it means you're in charge of what happens *in* you.

7. What fear doesn't want you to know is that it has no power over you outside of what it has already made you believe—so it has no power in the *present* moment, only in the past.

8. Darkness has no name, no face, other than the one we put on it.

9. Do future fears ever come or is our worry their arrival?

10. You would never have to sell yourself for a future happiness if you would work right now to refuse a present unhappiness.

Chapter 10

The Wonder Of My Mind

The Wonder Of The Mind

After seeing birds fly free through wide open skies, the mind had to know the secret of flight. When it saw the sorrow and suffering of human disease, the same mind sought to discover the real causes and cures. And when it gazed up into the star-filled night, there was no holding it back until we could look down upon ourselves from the heavens above. And this makes me Wonder ...

... Given all of the worlds into which the questions of the mind have reached, breached and tamed, why isn't the mind more interested in why it still doesn't know the secret of itself?

Add These Insights To Your Wonder About The Mind

1. A divided mind has many options, but no resting place.

2. It is a Spiritual Law that the purposeful and persistent investigation of your own mind will lead you to a New Mind— where your greatest enduring pleasure will be that you now *know* your Self.

3. There really are no obstacles for the mind that awakens to an understanding of itself, while the mind that lingers asleep and in the dark must forever run into itself.

If we work marble, it will perish; if we work upon brass, time will efface it; if we rear temples, they will crumble into dust; but if we work upon immortal minds and instill into them just principles, we are then engraving upon tablets which time will not efface, but will brighten and brighten to all eternity.

—Daniel Webster

The Wonder Of Self Certainty

There are those who say nothing is Sacred; they are certain there is no God. No evidence lays before their eyes. They have looked and found no signs; searched and made no contact. But remember, there are also those who have lost their keys—in their own home— and haven't been able to find them anywhere. And this makes me Wonder ...

... Could it be when we can't find the object of our search, whatever its nature—High or low—it's because we're so certain we know where to look?

Add These Insights To Your Wonder About Self Certainty

1. Nothing conspires to defeat
   so thoroughly as self certainty
   when once complete.

2. Whenever we've lost something important, *our memory searches itself* for the most
   certain places to look; but what is Sacred,
   what is Ever-New, will never be found in
   memory.

3. Unhappiness and self certainty are secret
   lovers who have made it a strict rule never
   to be seen in each other's company.

*All men who know not where to look for
truth save in the narrow well of self,
will find their own image at the bottom
and mistake it for what they are seeking.*

—J.R. Lowell

The Wonder Of Indecision

We have all felt that secret, strained concern over the need to go ahead and make some important decision in our life. Our pain is that we'd rather not have to choose at the moment—and while we know that our course of inaction isn't going to make us feel any better—at least from the relative safety of this position we're not going to make the *wrong* choice. And this makes me Wonder ...

... If the root of indecision is fear, then isn't indecision itself a mistake?

Add These Insights To Your Wonder About Indecision

1. There is such a thing as choosing *not* to decide when *you know that you don't know;* but this is very different from living with the conflict of indecision where you think you do know the right choice ... but are too afraid to choose.

2. Better to live and learn the hard way—if that's what it takes—than never learn to live at all.

3. Indecision is always the unconscious decision to live in conflict and in fear, so just go *through it* ... on the other side of the resistance is the flow.

To be always intending to live a life, but never to decide to set about it, this is as if a man should put off eating, drinking and sleeping from one day to another, til he is starved and destroyed.

—John Tillotson

The Wonder Of Purpose

Without some clear and constant purpose before our inner eyes, life is simply spent for us; our vital forces wasted serving aboard a mental ship with no captain at the helm; where instead of being able to choose our own destination, we're carried along by the winds and whims of our own uncharted mind ever searching for it knows not what. Until, too late, our supplies all but run out, we're forced to make landfall in some shallow harbor not of our choosing. And this makes me Wonder ...

... If the mind keeps on working and moving when you've asked it to be still, whose work is it doing and for what purpose?

Add These Insights To Your Wonder About Purpose

1. When your One Great Purpose in this life is to know yourself, then every wind is at your back—and every harbor holds a treasure.

2. Without attention there is no discernment; and without the ability to discern the futile from the fruitful, any distraction that fills our senses seems a suitable purpose.

3. The purpose of your mind is to serve you in the incredible thought-stopping discovery that *it* can't know the True Purpose of your life.

The man who seeks one, and but one, thing in life may hope to achieve it; but he who seeks all things, wherever he goes, only reaps from the hopes he sows, a harvest of barren regrets.
—Edward Bulwer-Lytton

The Wonder Of Turning To Learning

Whenever painful events happen, they tend to fall on only one of two sides of a person. The first side is the denial side. When turning this way, refusal rules. Regret, self pity and endless explanations generally follow. Or, the life blow falls on the angry side where the turning is to burning. Resentment rages. Hatred and feelings of betrayal mushroom into self righteous plans for avenging the wrong. But what both these sad sides have in common is that they keep the person between them a victim—turning in vain from one side to the other—only to find nothing changes except for the kind of pain found there. And this makes me Wonder ...

... Where do painful events fall on us when we decide on turning to our learning side?

Add These Insights To Your Wonder About Turning To Learning

1. You are a Living Instruction that calls out to be studied, applied, and realized.

2. Self education is self courage, since 99% of what frightens us is what we find out about ourself a moment too late.

3. Some of the highest lessons of all are learned without having to think about them at all—as in the discovery that it's perfectly all right to run out of thoughts.

The most useful piece of learning for the uses of life is to unlearn what is untrue.
—Antisthenes

The Wonder Of Change

On one hand, everyone agrees that change is the one true constant in this life—and that in our willingness to meet it openly—we acquire a certain suppleness of spirit that can be gained in no other way. Like the sapling that strengthens as it learns to bend in fickle winds, change forms us in the wisdom of its ways. And yet, for all of this, with our other hand we firmly resist and often resent change. We want nothing to do with it unless it promises to take us in the direction of our plans. So it seems we want change *only as long as it doesn't change what we want*. And this makes me Wonder ...

... Other than rearranging those things we want, what does it mean to really change?

Add These Insights To Your Wonder About Change

1. Running out of ideas about how to change yourself is the first real step towards a brand new you.

2. Meeting increasing resistance in our work to be new doesn't signal the limits of our capacity for change, but heralds only the threshold to the next level of a Higher self understanding—which already belongs to us if we'll enter.

3. When you know, deeply, that everything changes, then you also know that nothing in this life can really be *for* you or *against* you ... and then all is Well *within* you.

> *The greatest and most important problems of life are all in a certain sense insoluble ... They can never be solved but only outgrown.*
>
> —Carl Jung

The Wonder Of Defeat

The real victory over this life isn't found in this or that achievement, but in overcoming our belief in defeat. Having once defeated the darkness of defeat, we are never again visited by any of its idiot associates—as in the likes of fear and despair. But this battle for self mastery is an inner one—for *defeat is not a fact of life*, it's only a confused *feeling* about it. And more than that, these mistaken feelings of futility are entirely unnecessary because *nothing* can stop us from starting over! So feeling defeated is the culmination of a dark self deception—where it's our own thoughts telling us—"it's too late to change the way things are"—that make it that way. And this makes me Wonder ...

... What if the only thing that continues to defeat us is our own unconscious wish to feel that way?

Add These Insights To Your Wonder About Defeat

1. Defeat is nothing but the *memory* of that moment when all that you knew couldn't get you through—so to really start out new, you need to first let go of you.

2. A thousand plans to get ahead are worth less than one insight into what's holding us back.

3. Courageously call into doubt any troubling thought or feeling that wants you to accept the inevitability of some unhappy condition.

> *What is defeat?—Nothing but education; nothing but the first step to something better.*
>
> —Wendell Phillips

The Wonder Of Self Doubt

There is a secret war within each of our hearts that wages hour on the hour. A silent battle, this siege of self doubt is the never ending wish to do what is right: Who to be ... What to do ... How to act—and with each new encounter, this challenge must be met. But cloaked ever so carefully within this wish to do true is our fear of being wrong. And it's always on a restless march. So though we may not see it, the evidence is clear. We are both sides of the assault. And this makes me Wonder ...

... How can you win a war when *you* are the battle?

Add These Insights To Your Wonder About Self Doubt

1. Self doubt is built into thinking about ourself, because each of these thoughts contains its own unseen opposite which accordingly calls itself into question.

2. Firmly determine when faced with any self doubt that *you* will either resolve it or drop it, but under no circumstance will you let *it* give you an answer.

3. One simple guideline for finding yourself in any crowd of conflicting thoughts or feelings is to remember right in their midst *that you are none of them.*

> *Nothing can make you sure of yourself but the self you really are.*
> —Vernon Howard

The Wonder Of Starting Over

Events demand decisions. Choices must be made. And we do the best we know how in any given moment. Even so, we often err and choose against ourself. For a split second we sense our misstep and would we could put things right, but the momentum of the moment holds us helpless in its tow. Seemingly too late to struggle with what has now been cast, we can only hope tomorrow won't find us on some unpleasant shore. But in truth, there is no grim tide of events to which we must submit. It's only our flooding thoughts that carry us along. And we can start life all over any time we'll remember that nothing *real* keeps us from standing on Solid Ground. And this makes me Wonder ...

... Where is it written we must surrender our life and be held captive of any conflict or painful regret?

Add These Insights To Your Wonder About Starting Over

1. Nothing—and everything—is inevitable, as long as we're willing to start over until our course is changed.

2. The newness of now has no opposites and therefore *never knows opposition*—which is why your sincere wish to start over cannot help but succeed.

3. Merely thinking about starting over isn't a new beginning any more than reading a book on climbing mountains is the deep breath of fresh air that only comes with being there.

Lose no time, get up and take the course again, for he who rises quickly and continues his race makes it as if he had never fallen.

—Miguel Molinos

The Wonder Of Not Knowing

Embracing a new pain to remedy an old one, like worrying over growing doubts, is not the proof we know what to do with our pain. Just the opposite holds true. Mental or emotional pain proves that we don't know what to do—because if we understood the conflict—we wouldn't still have the hurt. So when we meet any moment that's mixed with fear or some kind of dread, these shaky inner states are signposts meant to be read. And what they are trying to tell us is, "Wait right here until the way is clear. The road's out just ahead." And this makes me Wonder . . .

. . . How many times do we have to come to that moment when it's clear we don't know what to do—before we learn to stop right there instead of jumping ahead into the painful pretense that we do?

Add These Insights To Your Wonder About Not Knowing

1. The pain of knowing that we don't know what to do is only entered once, while the pain of pretending that we do understand lives on for as long as the pretense.

2. There are one thousand ways *out* of what is True, but only one way *in* to It.

3. If we'll learn to live without telling ourself who we are—and without knowing what to do about our pain—the day will arrive when we'll have seen so much about what's hurting us, we just won't look to it anymore for who we are.

> *What is the use of going right over the old track again? ... You must make tracks into the unknown.*
> —Henry David Thoreau

Review These Ten Helpful Hints About The Wonder Of Your Mind

1. Invested attention returns perfect protection.

2. When you think, "I shouldn't be afraid, therefore I'm not," you are still in fear ... only dreaming you aren't.

3. Waiting for your invitation into your life is a Nature that never thinks about itself.

4. Attention is the anchor of Now.

5. A rolling thought gathers mass.

6. Whenever we fiercely declare, "No one will ever hurt me again," we just did to ourself what we don't want others to do.

7. Recovering from a sorry situation is not the same as revealing what brought it to you in the first place.

8. The first discovery that our awakening attention makes is that we've never had any real attention.

9. The joy in encountering something greater than our present understanding is, that with our persistent wish to understand it, comes the release of our present understanding—which must always precede any True New Understanding.

10. Light doesn't answer the darkness—it cancels it.

Chapter 11

The Wonder Of Letting Go

The Wonder Of The Unexpected

For most of us, the very best we could hope to happen each moment of our lives would be to give ourselves what we think we must have to be happy. And this makes me Wonder ...

... What if life has something Higher in mind *it* would like to give us in those moments?

Add These Insights To Your Wonder About the Unexpected

1. You can spend your life forcing it to go *your* way, or you can give up your life to The Way, and let it show you its lasting contentment.

2. What is truly New can only arrive on its terms—for if your terms determine its moment of arrival, there is nothing new about it.

3. Falling in love with the unexpected is the same as learning to fall in love with life.

The life of every man is a diary in which he means to write one story, and writes another; and his humblest hour is when he compares the volume as it is with what he hoped to make it.

—James M. Barrie

The Wonder Of Negative Reactions

It seems to me that we are almost always going through one thing or another. Someone says something we don't like or a difficult situation surfaces unexpectedly, and the next thing we know, the world suddenly seems a much darker place. And this makes me Wonder ...

... Is it really these EVENTS which block the sunlight from our skies, or is it our own dark REACTIONS to these events which turn them into personal eclipses?

Add These Insights To Your Wonder About Negative Reactions

1. When all is said and done, the way we are given to feel in any moment all comes down to what we love.

2. Solving ourself is the same as solving our sorrows.

3. There is only one thing that determines whether we are Master or slave of each moment—and that is our level of understanding.

> *Remember that it is not the man who gives blows or abuse who offends you, but the view you take of these things as being offensive. When, therefore, anyone provokes you, be assured that it is your own opinion which provokes you.*
>
> —Epictetus

The Wonder Of Learning Patience

Who among us can't count the times we've regretted reaching some premature, self wrecking conclusion—where not only were we wrong in our initial estimation of the event but then—in short measure—we also came to find that the very incident we had thought to be a bad tiding turned to be good? And this makes me Wonder ...

... In spite of all the lessons to the contrary, why do we still insist upon imposing our meaning onto life's events when, with just a bit of patience, they would be pleased to reveal their true meaning to us?

Add These Insights To Your Wonder About Learning Patience

1. We are so quick to be against ourselves and so slow to see it.

2. While there are times it may be true that "he who hesitates is lost", it's almost always true that he who can *wait* seldom loses himself.

3. Patience places us outside the clock of our *own* creation and there teaches us, in its time, the Wonder of God's creation.

Trust to God to weave your thread into the Great Web, though the pattern shows it not yet.

—George MacDonald

The Wonder Of Self Punishment

When someone is angry with you, your own awakened insight shows you he isn't really angry at *you*, but only with his fixed *idea* about you. Something unexpected in your behavior has upset his mental picture of you—and *its* wavering shape is making *him* feel like he's losing control. So he reasons wrongly it's you on the attack—and the only choice left for him is to return the attack. And his conviction you're to blame is confirmed with his every strike, for the pain he gives is the pain he then gets—since all he really rages against is an image within his own mind which is where each of his blows finds its mark. And this makes me Wonder . . .

. . . What need is there to punish those who would punish us—when they have already been so thoroughly self punished?

Add These Insights To Your Wonder About Self Punishment

1. The mind can never "build a case" against someone else without first having encased itself.

2. The first experience we have of any event is always that of ourself.

3. The very worst punishment of all is to remain someone who never realizes that he or she is a self punishing machine.

Do not usurp thy Makers place by giving way to wrath—wrath that goes forth in vengeance; "vengeance is mine, I will repay, saith the Lord."
—Charles Simmons

The Wonder Of Seeking Answers

There's no end to the answers we can find when looking for ways to free ourself from personal problems. But the fact that few of these have ever worked eludes our attention, because as quickly as each of these self saving solutions collapses, another rushes in to take its place. In fact, we've become dependent upon this constant inner exchange of answers—for it fuels an ever-shifting sense of purpose which gives us a certain false sense of self. And so certain are we in the intelligence of this seeking self, it never enters our mind to question any of our own questions; questions whose only purpose seems to be to keep us ever on the search. And this makes me Wonder ...

... Is there any answer that can ever resolve a compulsive question, or is the only answer to see that there isn't—and then just drop the question?

Add These Insights To Your Wonder About Seeking Answers

1. Never fear the temporary absence of a recognizable answer because on the other side of that fear is freedom from the tormenting question; the Higher Answer your heart seeks.

2. You are the answer; don't seek it elsewhere.

3. Nothing we can ever imagine can compare with what God has in mind for us.

The first point of wisdom is to discern that which is false; the second to know what is true.

—Lactantius

The Wonder Of Pressure

In olden days long gone by, sailors and whal-
ers far out at sea, would sometimes have to
take to their longboats to row—their wooden
ships in tow—in search of a favorable breeze.
And it was persistence coupled with their
aching hands and weary arms that would
put them in the right place to be when the
winds finally shifted from being in their
faces to at their backs. But we are not makers
of the wind. It blows when and where it
pleases. It can be known, but never owned;
expected, but never commanded. And there
are none who can sail against the wind. And
this makes me Wonder ...

... Where's the pressure in this life if we
aren't pushing against the wind?

Add These Insights To Your Wonder About Pressure

1. Outside of who you *think* you have to be, there is no other pressure.

2. Our feeling of being powerless is proportionate to our insistence that things go the way we want them to go.

3. It's impossible to wish for any pleasure that doesn't carry within it an unseen pressure to consummate its enjoyment *before* its arrival ... and there's no pleasure in pressure.

A little consideration of what takes place around us every day would show us that a higher law than that of our will regulates events; that our painful labors are unnecessary and fruitless; and that only in our easy, simple, spontaneous action are we strong.

—Ralph Waldo Emerson

The Wonder Of Attention

Everything that makes life excellent depends on where we place our attention. Living as we usually do, with our minds eye fixed on what we'll one day be, or what we'll have or win, our eyes are ever looking to the *end* of things. And this is where we're betrayed. There's no such thing as a happy ending without a true beginning. And in order to have any true beginning, our attention has to be *there*—on the beginning; moment to moment, and not on the end. Otherwise, we don't see what *is*, but only what we want to be there—and heartaches are the sad stuff of such dreams. And this makes me Wonder ...

... If we attend to the true beginning of any one thing, won't the end take care of itself?

Add These Insights To Your Wonder About Attention

1. In any race, always remember
   long before you're done,
   it's in knowing where *each* foot falls
   that tells how well it's run.

2. Awakened attention is the heart of Intelligence, and Intelligence never chooses against itself.

3. The Kingdom of Heaven is the space between two thoughts—and attention is both ship and anchor to take and hold us there.

Our grand business is not to see what lies dimly at a distance, but to do what lies clearly at hand.

—Thomas Carlyle

The Wonder Of Self Contradiction

No one looks for unpleasant situations. But some can't be avoided. And at the moment of their unwanted arrival, we want quickly away from their disturbing presence. Our aim is clear: Put as much distance as we can between ourselves and the offending condition. But here's where it turns strange. Even as we walk away, we're mentally mapping the whole ugly event. And then, as soon as we can find a friend who will listen, we spill our sad story from start to finish—being careful not to omit any of the painful details. So even as we protest the just past bitter scene, we find ourselves drawn to relive it— over and over again. And this makes me Wonder ...

... Isn't there a contradiction in how much we love to talk about what we hate?

Add These Insights To Your Wonder About Self Contradiction

1. The only real remedy for painful self contradiction is increased consciousness.

2. Few are those who believe they don't understand themselves, which is why so many discover, too late, they've been compromised.

3. Self study is the foundation of self release.

Among the many contradictions in our nature, few are as glaring as this, between our sensitiveness to the slightest disgrace which we fancy cast upon us from without, and our callousness to what is wrong in ourselves. In truth, they who are the most sensitive to the one are often the most callous to the other.

—Anonymous

The Wonder Of Ambition

The story goes that when Alexander The Great sensed his time approaching to pass from this life, he tried in vain to battle back death and to close its dark door. But powerful as he was, nothing in his command would stay the Reapers' solemn course. So knowing well the destiny of this defeat, he gave instructions he was to be buried with his hands empty and open; palms facing up toward the sky. This was to show—for those who could see it—that for all he had conquered in this world, he had won nothing of any permanence. Too late he learned that time defeats all ambition. And this makes me Wonder ...

... Wouldn't it be wise to seek immortality?

Add These Insights To Your Wonder About Ambition

1. To have lived without ever knowing something of forever would be to have come upon the perfect rose and to have never known its fragrance.

2. Letting go of what you think you have to have to be happy is the same as letting go of the you that's never happy with what you have.

3. When we seek this world we win its gifts that are fashioned in time, but when we seek the Celestial we find ourselves—and that we've something within us which made the stars.

The slave has but one master, the ambitious man has as many as there are persons whose aid may contribute to the advancement of his fortune.
—Jean Bruyere

The Wonder Of Self Release

Most believe we can't let go of persistent self punishing states because certain feelings about people or past events are just too strong; that they somehow have a hold on us and so are beyond our power to release them. But this just isn't true. Thoughts and feelings have no arms or hands with which to hold us fast. If we can't drop some painful inner condition there's only one reason for it. Somewhere within, some unseen part of ourself is holding on—afraid to let go because its only life is in the clinging. And to release the pain, it would have to give itself up. And this makes me Wonder ...

... Why choose to know ourselves through some sadness, when nothing can keep us from letting go and quietly being no one?

Add These Insights To Your Wonder About Self Release

1. The secret of self release lies just beyond our unseen certainty that we have to be who we think we have to be.

2. Release yourself from self punishing dreams by seeing they do nothing except promise *future pleasures* while delivering only *present imprisonment*.

3. Cooperate with your own release by refusing to be satisfied with anything less than 100% spiritual freedom.

> *There is provided an escape from the narrowness and poverty of the individual life, and the possibility of a life which is other and larger than our own, and yet which is most truly our own. For, to be ourselves, we must be more than ourselves. What we call love is, in truth ... the losing of our individual selves to gain a larger self.*
>
> —John Caird

A Special Summary To Help You Wonder And Let Go

1. Learning to let go of yourself is the same as learning to be happy.

2. Go on with your life as though no one is coming.

3. One way to avoid at least a few unpleasant conversations is to never again talk to *yourself*.

4. Just because something is persistent doesn't mean it's intelligent ... as in worried thoughts and feelings.

5. Fear can never choose other than in favor of itself.

6. Remember, most people are not trying to row the boat, they're trying to sink it.

7. When faced with an impassable life situation, letting go of what you *think* you know is the same as letting go of the impasse—because you wouldn't be blocked if you weren't so sure you knew the only way.

8. Why is it always easier to see that someone else is a prisoner of their own making.

9. You can no more put life on hold than you can hold onto your own life.

10. To start life over requires authentic self release, which is why so many stop short of receiving a new life.

Chapter 12

The Wonder Of Wonder

The Wonder Of Silence

Given that intelligence can only be measured by a countless number of factors, some of which include—but are not limited to—the power to perceive, the ability to understand, and the awareness of relationship—then wouldn't the Highest Order of Intelligence be that lofty state which allows for the greatest number of these possibilities all at once? And that makes me Wonder ...

... Wouldn't a *silent* mind best fulfill this special condition?

Add These Insights To Your Wonder About Silence

1. Everything is New to silence.

2. This is the strong safety of a silent mind: There is nothing which can ever enter into some silence without first having to break it—and so in this way is every visitor announced.

3. Silence is that silver cup
   which life fills over and over again
   without ever filling up.

> *What a strange power there is in silence. How many resolutions are formed, how many sublime conquests effected, during that pause when lips are closed and the soul secretly feels the eye of her maker upon her.*
> —Ralph Waldo Emerson

The Wonder Of Resistance

Tell some men and women that their weakness doesn't belong to them and watch how they act as though you're trying to take something from them they need. It's clear they somehow secretly value this weakness. What isn't so obvious is why anyone wants to hold onto what is weak. Here's a surprising answer. Almost the only kind of strength these individuals have ever known is how strongly they feel about *not wanting to be weak*—even though this kind of strength has never rescued them from anything. And this makes me Wonder ...

... Is our strong resistance to some self weakness really a separate strength—a power that will one day prevail—or is this resistance only a hidden part of the very thing it resists?

Add These Insights To Your Wonder About Resistance

1. For every action there is an equal and opposite reaction which is why Christ said, "Resist not evil."

2. What if *not wanting to feel* what you're feeling at the moment is the feeling you don't want?

3. There can be no real self change as long as who we want to become is born out of who we no longer want to be—because each of our seemingly new self images has its origin within its opposite—*and opposites attract!*

> *Resistance to the disturbance is the disturbance.*
>
> —Vernon Howard

The Wonder Of Color And Light

Whenever sunlight touches upon the open face of a wildflower, the yellow and golden glow our eyes can see is just that small portion of the whole light spectrum that has not been absorbed by the outstretched petals. It's only that part of the light the flower *can't* absorb which is reflected back—and that's what we call its color. Now consider that these laws concerning color and light hold true with every thing—and that nothing is seen in the light of all the colors that it is—but only for those colors *that it isn't*. And this makes me Wonder ...

... In what light do we need to stand to see someone's TRUE color?

Add These Insights To Your Wonder About Color and Light

1. If we could, for only a moment, just see ourself in the same light with which we are so quick to look upon others, we would soon know that that light has never been but a darkness, and never again would we cast its unforgiving shadow across another.

2. None are safe who won't see all of the colors they are, while there is no danger for those who will stand unafraid of and fully in the Light.

3. There is a Light lingering within the heart that sees life without seeing what is in it as being worlds apart.

Light is the shadow of God.

—Plato

The Wonder Of Self Surrender

Although many profess it otherwise, heart-ache and disappointment are not the bitter fruits of expectations turned sour. It's true these sad states seem to surface even as our hopes start sinking, but they are *not* the effects of any particular missed moment. These daily upsets in life persist because we don't remember one essential and indisputable fact: While there's almost no limit to what we can do with our intellect—with its immense powers for imagining and implementing our own intricate self perfected plans—we've forgotten that our mind does not govern the Intelligence that created it. And this makes me Wonder ...

... Why can't we remember that before we are creators of this life, we ourselves are special creations within it?

Add These Insights To Your Wonder About Self Surrender

1. Find the direction the Intelligence of this life is moving and then surrender what you must until you feel it lift and begin to carry you.

2. The paradox of self surrender is that as we learn to submit to the Order of Life, we are freed from the fear of it—and so find the very self command we had been seeking.

3. Self surrender is not the acceptance of our limitations, but the only true way to transcend them.

> *Liberty in submission—what a problem! And yet, this is what we must always come back to.*
>
> —Henri Amiel

The Wonder Of Evil

Evil wants us to believe there's no such thing as evil. But there is. And whenever we suspect its wicked presence, evil wants us to be afraid of our suspicion and to look the other way. It knows its only hope is to stay unconfirmed—because without a place to hide, evil has no place to reside. So it has learned ways to insure we turn our eyes away. It knows we'd rather not face fear—so fear is the face it wears. But evil is *nothing* without its mask of fear and body of deceptions. They serve one another as the thief is served by a lightless night. And this is the curse that evil will never escape: Unless it dwells in darkness, evil has no dwelling at all. And this makes me Wonder ...

... What is evil other than what we've yet to uncover within ourselves?

Add These Insights To Your Wonder About Evil

1. Just as darkness has no power over the light of even one candle, so too is evil powerless to turn us away from our task of self illumination.

2. We are not the creator of evil, but in trying to hide its presence, we then become its possessor ... and its possessed.

3. The bright day must come—if you'll persist with your wish to Wonder—when you'll be able to say to any evil, "darkness, I laugh in your face!"

Many have puzzled themselves about the origin of evil. I am content to observe that there is evil, and that there is a way to escape it, and with this I begin and end.

—John Newton

The Wonder Of Emptiness

If we'd only examine those moments when our life seems suddenly empty, we'd see this emptiness always arrives with the departure of something which we were certain had been giving our life *meaning*. A relationship fades, the future dims, or a promise breaks— and feelings of emptiness follow behind. We sense our life as being temporarily meaning-less and that our awful *inner* emptiness is somehow connected. And it is; but *not* in the way we presently think. Our emptiness never eases because Life already has its own meaning ... which we carelessly cover up each and every time we make the mental mistake of naming it for ourself. And this makes me Wonder ...

... Is the reason we feel so empty, so often, because we keep on doing empty things?

Add These Insights To Your Wonder About Emptiness

1. Emptiness is that friendly beacon in the night of our spirit—shining on to show us that nothing of *this* world can fill us up.

2. People with nothing more important to do than to waste their own lives will always try to get you involved in what they're doing.

3. Emptiness is the feeling that follows the mistake of looking to the temporary for the Eternal.

> *The wish falls often, warm upon my heart, that I may learn nothing here that I cannot continue in the other world; that I may do nothing here but deeds that will bear fruit in heaven.*
> —Jean Paul Richter

The Wonder Of Strength

Weakness is never something we expect from ourself. It just seems to appear out of nowhere with its horrible host of unwelcome characteristics. Weakness places us at the mercy of any angry face or compulsive desire, and then keeps us explaining ourselves to ourselves, and to anyone else who demands to know why we're alive. And we always feel badly after we've been so weak, because this helps us to feel better! These habitual sentiments seem to tell us we had a choice; that we could have been strong if we really wanted to. So we start to believe that one of our strengths is how sorry we can feel for having been weak. But real Strength is the absence of weakness, not our excuses for it. And this makes me Wonder ...

... What if our real weakness is that we don't know what true Strength is, but only think we do?

Add These Insights To Your Wonder About Strength

1. It's healthy to ask ourselves, each time one of our weaknesses arrives on the scene, why *none* of our strengths are anywhere to be found!

2. Weak thoughts and feelings often *feel* strong, but remember, real Strength is *never* anxious, cruel, or punishing.

3. The one Strength that never turns into its unhappy opposite is the true Self Understanding that you are not, and have never been, your weakness.

> *God never makes us sensible of our weaknesses, except to give us of His strength.*
>
> —Francis Fenelon

The Wonder Of Invisible Influences

Invisible influences are the building blocks of visible life. Some of these familiar influences, such as gravity and temperature, actually shape the world we see. The unique forms of trees, birds and bees are all natural expressions of these unseen forces. But these physical life-forms can only bear silent witness to the shapes they must take. They have no voice, no choice in the image they are fashioned. But *we can choose*. Ours is the power to know what moves upon and within our Self. This Consciousness *is* choice. And from it we may embrace—or reject—any influence, cosmic or human—and in doing so, choose the image in which our Being is formed. And this makes me Wonder ...

... What invisible influences are shaping us even right now?

Add These Insights To Your Wonder About Invisible Influences

1. The power of attention is self command ... for without it we may be influenced to choose against ourself ... and never have possessed the presence of mind to notice our loss.

2. The influence and safety of Inner Light isn't so much what it can do, as it is what *can't* be done in its presence.

3. We profit or lose not by what we do with each moment, but by what we love in it— for we are influenced first by our own heart which, in turn, is influenced by a greater one.

Always act so that the immediate motive of thy will may become a universal rule for all intelligent beings.
—Immanuel Kant

The Wonder Of Being Special

Most of us want to be special, which makes us common. The difference between *being* special and *wanting* to be special is the difference between living on top of a mountain or under one. The only thing special about human beings who want to be special is the special kind of pain they live with to prove to themselves they are. Trying to be special is like trying to be a human being. We already are human—so the more we struggle to prove it, the less of one we seem in our own eyes, as well as in the eyes of others. Don't *try* to be special. Instead, *be awake to who you really are*. What is special will follow. And this makes me Wonder ...

... Wouldn't a truly special person be the one who has no need to be seen as special at all?

Add These Insights To Your Wonder About Being Special

1. When at last you decide you'd rather find your own way, you will also find you have found yourself.

2. To the contrary, suffering doesn't prove how special we are, only how self gullible; otherwise we'd never believe there's something special about feeling dark and sorry.

3. See through and let go of your wish to be special and on the other side of your fear of being no one, you'll find a special New Nature that is forever yours.

He is great who is what he is from nature, and who never reminds us of another.

—Ralph Waldo Emerson

The Wonder Of The Truth

There is no Truth so great or distant that it can't be known—for just as the stream is guided to the sea, so does our sincere intention to know what is True lead us to the deep inlets of Timeless Understanding. And there are no mysteries here. Truth's Way *is* there, we may be assured. The first footfall is just as near to us as is our wish to be Truthful. We need only look to ourselves for its gate. Nothing obscures its view. The Truth is here, *now*, right before our eyes. There can be no other time for its place and no other place to find it. And this makes me Wonder ...

... If the Truth doesn't hide itself from us, do we hide the Truth from ourselves?

Add These Insights To Your Wonder About The Truth

1. Refuse to fear any Truth, no matter how frightening its fleeting appearance, and that Truth will make you fearless—which is what it means to be free.

2. The discovery of one small leak in the ship of your life is worth more than a thousand dreams of a safe crossing.

3. Truth is a cup which we must drink alone, but one which is raised to our lips by all those who have gone before us.

Keep one thing forever in view—the Truth; and if you do this, though it may seem to lead you away from the opinions of men, it will assuredly conduct you to the throne of God.

—Horace Mann

Ten Secret Principles To Strengthen Your Wish To Wonder

1. Rightness naturally rises.

2. No teaching can ever express Truth's sentiment because Truth is a presence—and teachings, no matter how sublime, are always a pathway from the past.

3. There is a triumph in any true beginning.

4. The evils of this world promise protection from the evils of this world.

5. As we learn to let life lead, we also discover it knows where we need to be.

6. The collapse of the opposites comes when you see that there is no hope in resistance.

7. If you want to please God, you must incur the wrath of the gods.

8. You can't have a fear that you don't first name.

9. Being lost is part of any true explorer's pleasure.

10. On one hand we demand too much—that life should answer to our desires; but on the other hand, we ask for far too little—for life wants more for us than we dare to dream.

Chapter 13

The Secret Well Of Wonder Within You

It had long been spoken of in certain circles of men that there existed a vast but hidden valley somewhere in the upper reaches of a great and not too distant mountain. Tales were told that within this remote and almost invisible gash in the side of the mountain, a seeker might find his fortune in precious gems and rare jewels; that is, *if* that seeker could somehow manage to survive there long enough to unearth their secret hiding places.

It seemed that not only was the valley a cold, almost waterless and wind-swept high-mountain desert, but some spoke of it as being heartless too. Fierce bandits patrolled the lower ranges; bad men who would swoop down onto unsuspecting, ill-prepared seekers, like vultures onto fresh carrion.

But these rumors and all of their rumors had no meaning to one man whose life had already begun to stop making sense to him anyway. And as he prepared to enter the valley he thought to himself it really didn't make too much difference what the future held. This was what life had lead him to and this was where he would either find his heart's content or lose his life trying.

He camped that night near the entrance of the valley perched in some out-cropping rocks and ridges. Here and there out in the bleak, black expanse before him, he could see little dots of light from distant campfires. But that evening came and went uneventfully. No one and nothing disturbed his sleep besides his own fitful dreams.

The next day he started his work of slowly sifting through the thousands of odd little stones that had trickled their way down a small stream to the foot of a catch bed. As he worked there he could see—contrary to the stories he had heard—there was water in the valley—but it was seasonal. His best guess gave him less than two weeks before the stream he had found would dry up ... and he figured the same would have to hold true everywhere else in the valley. He looked around and wiped the sweat from his face with his bare arm. This was a harsh place. Hardly anything grew here that hadn't been twisted by the constant winds, brittled by the heat, or born bristling with thorns.

He shook his head as if to shake off a bad dream and spoke out loud to himself, "Man, what in the name of God am I doing out here?" But the sound of his voice immediately disappeared into the waves of heated stillness like water into desert sands. He felt immensely alone.

The next week of evenings passed quickly. But

between his steadily increasing fatigue and the fact that more and more prospectors seemed to be setting up camp in the valley, he didn't know whether he should try and get some sorely needed sleep or work even harder. He decided on work. It was a terrible situation. He was too tired to press on and too anxious not to. After all, what if someone else found the motherload of gems before he did? Speaking of which—what steps should he take to try and protect the few precious stones he'd already come upon? His racing mind only made matters worse and he knew it. He could feel his remaining strength ebb from his body. And he was so thirsty.

His passed his tongue over his lips and they were parched. To make matters worse, the streams in the valley were all but gone now and more than once he had heard the sounds of fighting coming from the few remaining nearby pools. He was right in the middle of considering his whole situation when he was struck by a peculiar idea. Sure, it would delay his quest for riches, but if it were possible—if his scheme actually paid off—he would have a constant source of clean, life-giving water. He would dig a well for himself. He liked the idea even better the second time it passed through his mind. He would dig a well for himself. His own well. But where to dig it?

So early that evening in the cool of a slowly darkening sky, he set out away from the others to find the best-suited place to start digging for underground water.

That first night was the loneliest he could ever remember. Only the whispering of the wind spoke to his ears. He could hear nothing of the usual night sounds from the other side of the valley; those very sounds that used to irritate him. But now he found himself straining to hear them; the sounds of men whooping and yelling; of shots fired wild into the air; the brays of drunken men shouting out their good fortune or screaming in angry despair. But the wind carried no familiar voice other than its own. Nothing reached him. Nothing at all.

He began digging his well the next morning before the sun was up. It was hard going—nothing but rocks, one after another; big ones, small ones—just rocks and more rocks. He labored on for days. One night sitting by his campfire, the wind began whipping up the sand and dust as it always did at that hour. He wrapped his face in an old cloth and pulled down his hat, but the stinging sands still found their way through to his flesh. It was getting hard to breathe.

Finally, in a desperate attempt to find some shelter, he moved behind the huge pile of freshly unearthed rocks from his well's excavation. Peace at last. The winds couldn't lash him there. And that's just how it came to him. Why not build something out of all of these rocks? Maybe a small dwelling of some sort or at least some kind of permanent shelter? He was surprised he hadn't thought of it before but happy to have had the idea. Better late than never, he comforted himself.

During the next few weeks, alternating between digging in the well and sorting through the thousands of rocks, he built himself a small stone house.

The winds no longer reached him, but he had new problems to deal with. Underneath all the rocks he had found in the shaft of his would-be well, he had now encountered a loose, sandy kind of soil. Everything was unstable. His digging slowed to a crawl. Every foot of the well now had to be reinforced or the walls wouldn't hold. And there was the question of what to do with all of that soil that was piling up next to his house of rock.

He found his answer one afternoon during a particularly sorry lunch of dried biscuits, old beef jerky and a few remaining wild berries.

What wouldn't I give, he thought, for a carrot or a cabbage? Even a turnip? He mused. He hated turnips.

And as his mind dreamed of fresh vegetables, his eyes fell on all of the soil heaped up next to his pile of leftover boulders. Of course! He could build a garden bed walled by the rocks and then the winds wouldn't be able to blow the soil away!

So while he continued working on and digging in his well, he also worked at building sheltered garden beds. Each day he would take the soil from the well and fill the beds a little higher. And so it went. Each day deeper. Each day higher.

He began to love where he lived. He liked the quiet. He made friends with the animals that began coming around more and more. But still no water. And then every once in a while, he'd remember why he was out there on the mountain in the first place. He was supposed to be finding gems. It would startle him a bit that he could have forgotten. Those were the days that went on forever. And on those days he would dig extra hard; all the while talking to himself about how—once he had the water—he'd get right back to searching for his fortune.

Then one morning, his spade sliced through the bottom of the well with a strange ease. He dug again; and again. He could smell the moisture. Slowly, the deepest part of the newly exposed spade hole filled in with clear water. He reached down and cupped his hand. It was cold to the touch. And when he brought the water to his lips it was sweet; sweeter than anything he could ever recall.

He worked on a while longer pausing now and again to take a deep drink from the fruit of his labors. But he was having a hard time staying with the task at hand because he was starting to feel anxious. For a split second he thought maybe his anxiety was a sign; maybe something was telling him now that he had found water, he ought to get back to his original business of hunting treasure; maybe he ought to hurry up and get going. But no, that wasn't it. Clearly now he could see that wasn't it. He was feeling the way he was because he could hardly wait to take his first pail of water up to his new rock-wall garden—and then use it to plant his first seeds! And that's just what he did. Over and over again, all the rest of the day.

That night he slept as he had never before. And when he awakened, fully refreshed, he looked upon his garden, his well, and his little stone house and he knew he was never going to leave there. He had it all; a strong home; a source of fresh food; quiet, clear vistas and a well of wonderful water unlike any he had ever tasted. And although he couldn't have known it just then, the best was yet to come.

When he climbed back down to the bottom of the well to complete the digging and to finish shoring the sides, he couldn't believe his eyes. What had been just the night before only a small hole filled with a foot or so of water, was now a large seven foot pool filled with cool, clear water that came up to his shoulders! It was evident what had happened. As the underground waters seeped up overnight, they had eroded the sides of the well. The well was enlarging itself by itself! He couldn't believe his luck.

But wait! What was this? Something in the water near the outside edge of the bottom of the well caught his eye. Something glimmering. He reached down into the water and began slowly feeling his way along the sides. Could it be? Yes! He reached down again, and again, and each time his hand came up full. The bottom of the well was brimming with gems of all sizes. He laughed out loud. Nature had done for him—in one night—what he had never been able to do for himself. The gems and precious stones that had once been buried deep beneath those ancient soils had been freed when the upward seeping water collapsed the crusty walls of his well.

He laughed to himself this time. Somehow he always knew it would be this way. He didn't really care about the fortune that lay at his feet because he already had everything that he wanted. He had a home that couldn't be shaken or taken by any storm, whether assaulted by nature or man. And, he had all the water he would ever need to further transform his new mountain-high home into a totally self-sufficient safehold. He knew his wealth had no measure.

****

There is hidden in you, the reader, a secret well not unlike the amazing one in our story. And this is the Wonder of you. But, the Wonder of the well within you isn't just that it's self-replenishing—or that after a certain point it increases itself effortlessly—or even that it holds in its very foundation all the riches of this world. No. That's not it.

The Wonder of the well within you is that the moment you go to work on and within it—it will reveal—just as did the one in our story—that every one of its elements is actually a hidden part of your True Treasure. And that every seeming obstacle within it—within yourself; each hardened place and impasse, every impossible difficulty, every problem is transformed into a new power—once you know the Wonder of the well. This is a Living Well that knows what you need even before you ask. And the greatest Wonder of all is that because its very nature is Pure, High and Ever-Expansive, your life with and within it can be just the same. This is The Wonder Of The Well Within You.

Guy Finley lives and teaches in Ojai, California.

He invites you to let him know about your progress with Wonder.

Include a self-addressed, stamped envelope (#10-legal size) and receive his *free* Wonder Worksheet of additional valuable exercises, insights, and encouragement.

Send to: Guy Finley
              Box 1267 SW
              Ojai, CA 93024

Your Discoveries Are Your Healings

A Special Message From Vernon Howard

People do not know what their lives are all about. But sadly a false part inside them insists that it does understand. So people do not know that they do not know. Correct this. Just realize that your days are puzzles. If you really understood life would you have so may troubles? No. So honestly conclude that you are unaware of what is truly best for you. This is good. True knowing is already closer. Cosmic energy is working for you.

Only something else besides your present nature can understand these healing discoveries. Only a superior self can make Truth come alive with meaning and power. Attract this supreme nature by wanting it more than you want anything else in life. Strongly desire self-newness as you read along.

Here is the first step for winning mental and spiritual wholeness. You must admit your weaknesses and mistakes to yourself. This must be done many times each day. You must view your unsatisfactory life so bluntly that you are stunned by the power that harmful forces have over you. This bewildering dismay you have over your actual condition is a common and needful early encounter on the road to self- recovery. It is your first step, your first healing discovery.

But once you are conscious of your inner disorder you must immediately take the second step. It consists of a long and sustained effort to pass beyond the shock and discouragement you have found within yourself. I wish to repeat and emphasize that point. You must call upon spiritual powers to supply strength and endurance to travel beyond the appalling alarm you feel toward yourself. You must not linger with your self-dread. It will help you press forward to realize that a fascination with evil is a form of evil itself. People become spellbound by this wicked world, much like an animal on a dark highway is hypnotized by the headlights of an oncoming car.

The powers of darkness attack with full force at this critical moment in anyone's spiritual journey. It wants to prevent discovery from becoming healing. It fears your passage beyond your former nature. Bluffs and threats are some of the weapons it uses to keep the seeker in passive submission to its false power. Here are a few examples of the horrible hoaxes used by satanic spirits to keep you trapped: 1. Evil wants you to casually brush off the seriousness of your situation with the lie that things are not as bad as appears. 2. Evil lures humans into social and financial responsibilities and burdens not necessary in the first place. 3. Evil urges people to scream in rage against this sick world, knowing their fury keeps them tied to this world. 4. Evil makes people feel they are not loving or generous enough, causing them to relieve their false guilt with forced and artificial goodness. 5. Evil people sweet-talk you into giving them a helping hand, and when you do they steal part of your life while laughing at your gullibility.

Don't settle down with suffering! Resolve to travel on. Each time you do so you close off low-level influences and open yourself to high-level inspirations. This is a staggering blow against creepy creatures that want to hurt you. Now is the time for you to release heartache.

Suppose you are caught out in a raging storm. Your first urge is to fight your way out and get home. But the storm is so strong you forget your original aim and start fighting the storm itself. You feel encouraged when winning a small victory like finding a temporary hiding place. Hope then arises that you might survive the storm. That's hopeless. That's how most people go through life. You must remember that you are not supposed to endure the inner storm but get out of it altogether.

Let this spiritual exercise be a healthy discovery for you. It may sound strange at first, but stick with it. Tell yourself, "I will no longer *like* being unhealthy. I will no longer feel a strange fondness for an agitated life."

You may assume that you *already don't like* feelings of defeat and oppression. Think freshly. Make an effort to see that a certain part of you does in fact have a fondness for painful struggles. The reason the battle continues is precisely because you *have* allowed pain to control you. You can shock and scare this treacherous condition when you courageously declare, "I will no longer *like* being unhealthy." Discovery of a hidden burden creates new energy. It is another revelation for your elevation.

Villainous spirits do not want you to investigate them which is the perfect reason why you should. So be an eager student of the science of evilology which will actually purify your mind and actions. Just be true. Know that there is immense power in simply being right.

The first cause of evil and conflict is wicked spirits themselves. Evil originates with low and ungodly forces which are at first invisible but which then enter and control human bodies to create visible chaos such as crime. Keep in mind that the first cause of badness is cunningly concealed sinful spirits.

The second cause of conflict is the sleeping nature of a person which makes him follow wrongness as a way of life, which is really *unlife*. People are weak sheep who imitate observed evils. Ignorance serves sin. But wisdom serves peace, like freedom from embarrassing thoughts.

Evil tries to tighten its control over humans by smashing their reason and sanity. It wants you to remain in the state of helpless horror you have uncovered inside and outside yourself. These dark spirits even supply a certain thrill in being bad which you must recognize as a sly traitor to be dismissed.

Whoever corrects his ignorance about evil escapes the net tossed out by low forces. So he also escapes painful collisions as daily events. The higher always has power to push out the lower but *you* are the deciding factor. You must allow the Heavenly Spirit to do for you what it wants to do.

When feeling troubled there is always available to you a simple statement you can make that becomes your powerful helper. That statement is, "I need only pass beyond my present location." That says everything. Say it often. You will discover why you are here on earth.

Please understand that you now have a deep fear of the cunning world of darkness. But your fear is mostly unconscious, which means you don't understand how distress has possessed you to your terrible disadvantage. But have no concern over your confusion. Just remember that spiritual knowledge is your handy sword for defeating every fierce dragon.

Good and bad are in a power struggle. You take the power and let bad have the struggle.

Think of the most terrifying movie monster you have ever seen coming at you from the movie screen. Maybe it had flashing eyes and clutching claws. This is a movie, but this sort of scary scene is very much alive in the unexplored depths of people in real life. Outwardly a man or woman appears calm and successful but unseen terrors are really in command of what they do and feel. And they shake and shriek. They try in vain to hide their desperation from themselves and others.

Keep in mind: Secret suffering is still suffering. The movie monster took over your body and emotions. Yet, while one part of you trembled there was another part of you that knew it was just a movie. That separate section of yourself was not terrorized by the movie monster. Nothing bad was really happening to you.

Remember the phrase *"another part of you."* That separate self is your possession right now even though you do not yet understand or possess it for practical use. You always have a separate self that is never scared, never intimidated, never deceived. Your pleasure in life is to make permanent contact with the non-scared section of yourself. Its revelation is your salvation. Being within you at this very moment, it needs only your invitation for it to come stand strongly at your side. Invite your true essence to be your true life. Happiness is not when you *think* something but *are* something.

A spiritual student is like the owner of a large ranch who one day plants some trees in a remote corner of his property. He seldom visits the area. But one day years later he rides out that way and is delighted to see the trees displaying a wide variety of fruits and blossoms. Plant your spiritual seeds today. Tomorrow they will blossom. Your life will make perfect sense to you.

HELPFUL SUMMARY: 1. Honestly acknowledge negative features about your nature, then travel beyond yourself to a higher inner world. 2. Read these pages many times while giving deep thought to the meaning of the title, "Your Discoveries Are Your Healings."

A Wonderful Index For
Further Self Insight

For Additional Insights About . . .	Turn To These Wonders . . .
Self Love	Attachments (106) Individuality (64) Being Special (174) Resentment (84)
Self Newness	Unexpected (136) Resentment (84) Invisible Influ- ences (172) Useless Feelings (96)
Self Possession	Resentment (84) Change (124) Learning Patience (140) Purpose (120)
Self Protection	Turning To Learning (122) Resistance (160) Strength (170) Fear And Igno- rance (92)
Self Punishment	Resistance (160) Empty Apologies (88) Compassion (82) Negative Reaction (138)